TOTALLY DIABOLICAL

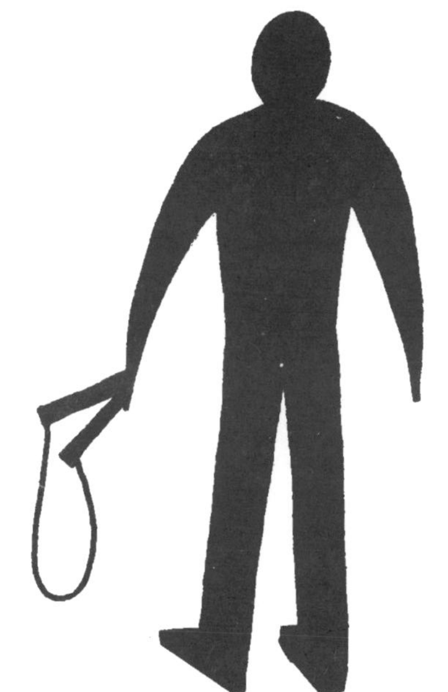

By Donald Grant

Illustrated by Donald Grant
Produced and Published by CIRCUSTUFF

ISBN 0 9520300 9 8

ISBN 0 9520300 9 8

Published by
CIRCUSTUFF
83 Uist Rd
Pitcoudie
Glenrothes
Fife
KY7 6RE
United Kingdom

Other CIRCUSTUFF Titles

By Donald Grant:

"My First Diabolo Book"
"Diabolo Stick Grinds and Suicides"
"Diabolo 2: Crazy Cradles and Baffling Body Moves"
"Diabolo 3: Two Hot to Handle" (with added Guy Heathcote)

"Stunning Starts and Fancy Finishes for Club Jugglers" by Doug
Dougal

"Mastering Devilstick (part one)" by Chris Dore

"Take 3 Clubs" by Robert Dawson

CONTENTS

INTRODUCTION

I wasn't going to write another one, I really wasn't; four books seemed to cover the subject *more* than adequately. Recent advances in diabolo technique have, however, made this book possible.

Contained within you shall find selections of the best new grinds, suicides, cradles and body moves. There's a bunch of awesome new two-diabolo tricks, plus a section on lots of weird and wacky alternative things.

For those of you who are interested in performing, I have also included pointers on a variety of different whipping techniques, driving and combinations, and a few hints on routine construction. There should be something in here for everyone, from the newly-converted to the true diabolunatic, for both pastimers and performers.

Of course, this still isn't *everything* possible in the world with a diabolo. Give it a few more years and who knows, perhaps all these tricks will have been superceded. Keep at it folks and maybe there'll be a sixth book in the trilogy. Until then, I hope you enjoy this one, as it's been a great pleasure to compile.

Anyway, don't just sit there ...

Donald Grant

THE STAR

A unique little cat's cradle, this one, as it can be performed literally with one hand behind your back.

1) Point both handsticks skywards.

2) Weave the left stick under the right string.

3) Then weave the right stick under the left string.

4) Pull tight, and this should be the result.

5) Now, put both handsticks together in one hand, holding them at a minimum of 90°, and turn them upside down. (NB: Any less than 90° and the cradle will simply slide off!)

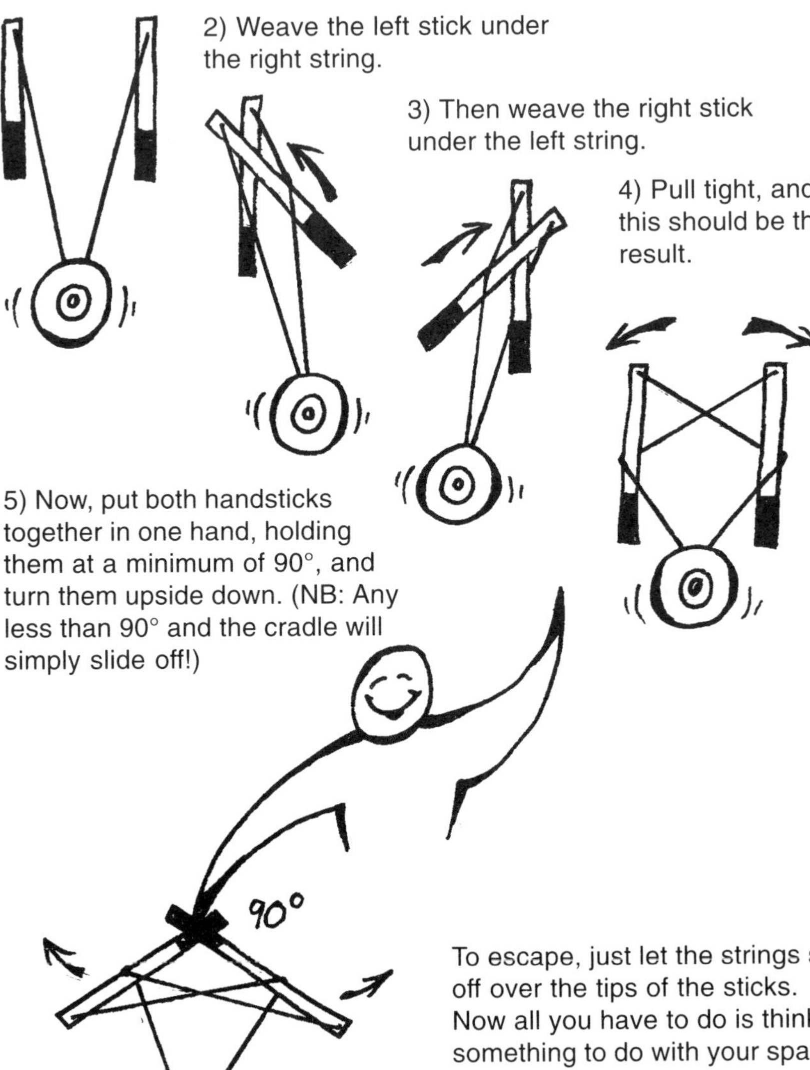

To escape, just let the strings slip off over the tips of the sticks. Now all you have to do is think of something to do with your spare hand. I'm sure you don't need any suggestions from the likes of me, do you?

CHINESE KNOT

The biggest and most incredible of all magic knots. Follow the instructions *very* carefully and it shouldn't be too much of a problem.

1) Turn your left handstick across your body, keeping it horizontal. Bring your right handstick around and over the front.

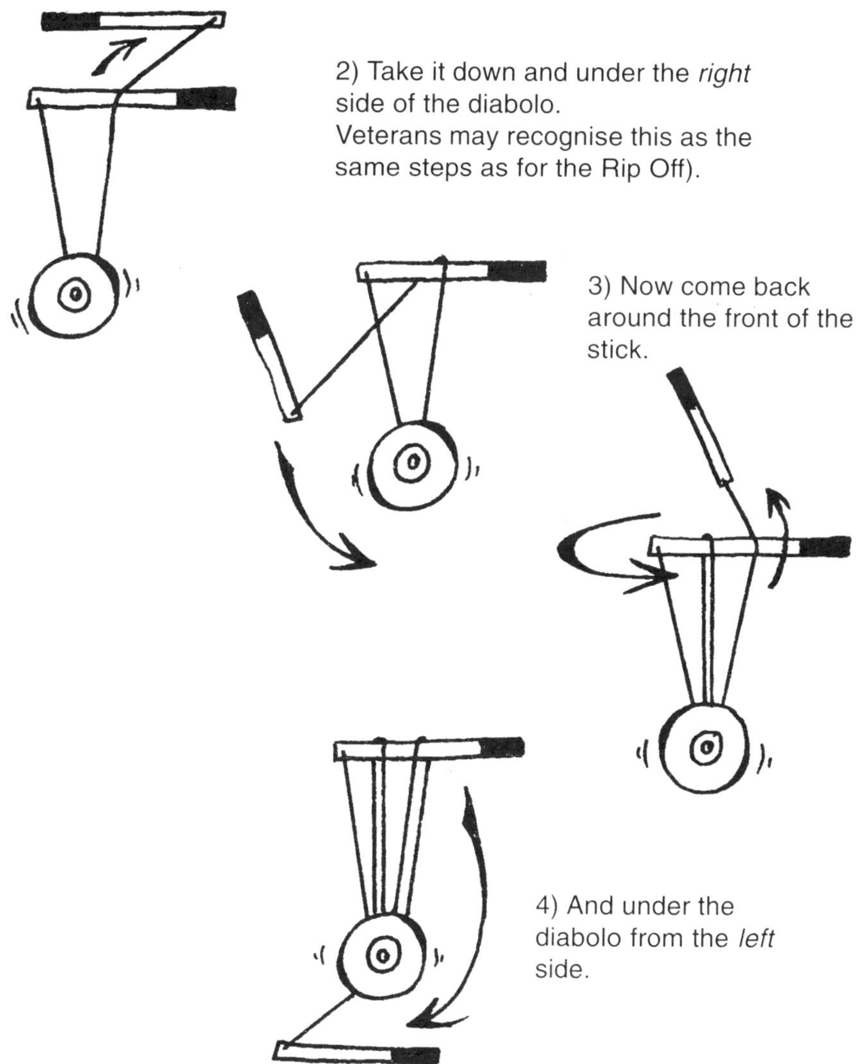

2) Take it down and under the *right* side of the diabolo.
Veterans may recognise this as the same steps as for the Rip Off).

3) Now come back around the front of the stick.

4) And under the diabolo from the *left* side.

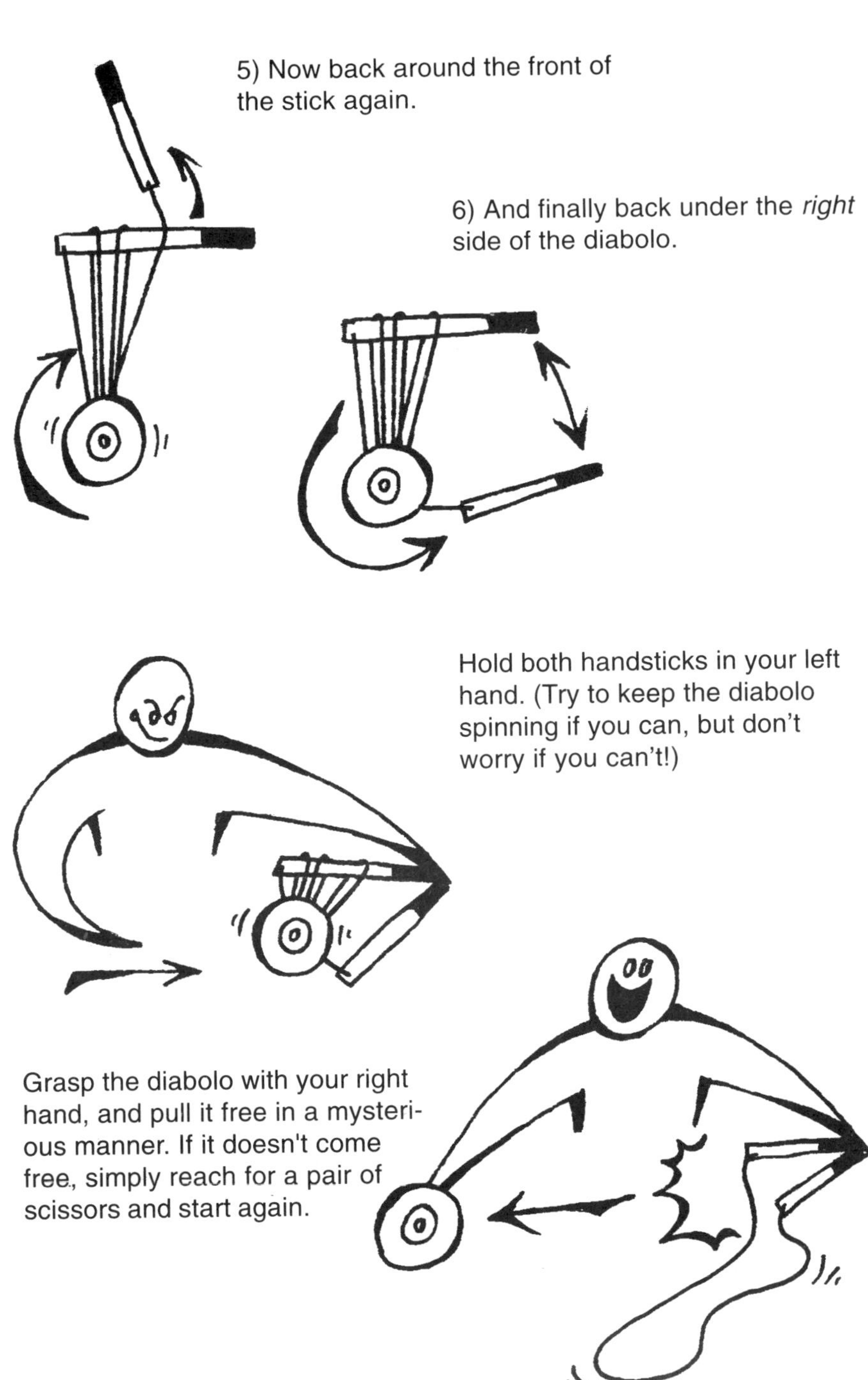

5) Now back around the front of the stick again.

6) And finally back under the *right* side of the diabolo.

Hold both handsticks in your left hand. (Try to keep the diabolo spinning if you can, but don't worry if you can't!)

Grasp the diabolo with your right hand, and pull it free in a mysterious manner. If it doesn't come free, simply reach for a pair of scissors and start again.

GRIND CARRY

A novel way to provide some variation in most boring old body moves.

1) While going around the leg, pop the diabolo straight up on the left side.

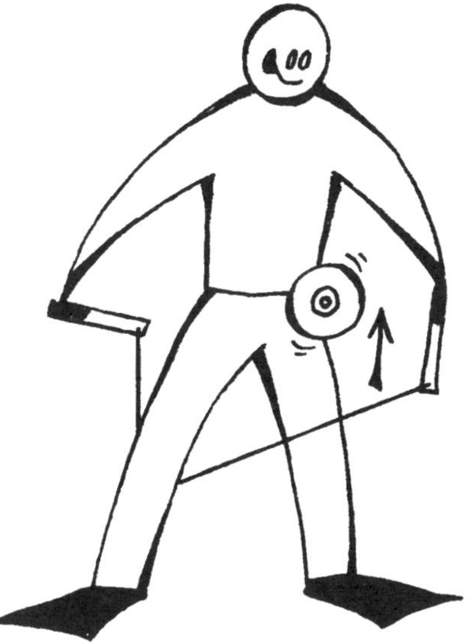

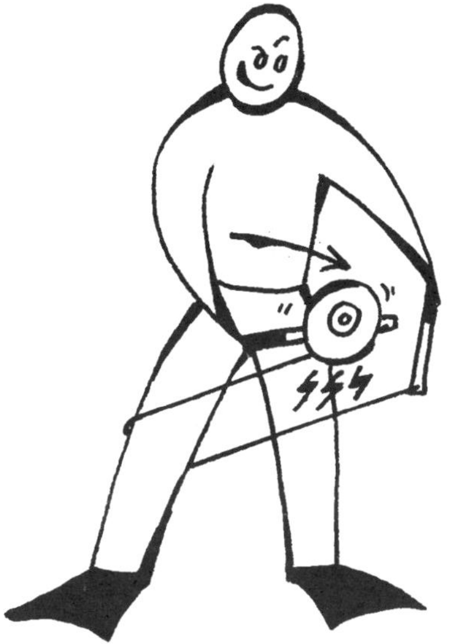

2) Reach across with your right handstick and catch the diabolo in a grind.

3) Carry the diabolo over to the right and tip it off back into around the leg.

This principle also works with figure of eight round the legs and behind the back moves. Or why not try putting a few stick switch grinds or rubberwrist catches in there as well? That ought to keep you busy for a while!

GRIND CURL

The hardest grind trick in the book. This is an awkward, body contorting move which demands the utmost in grind control. Even if you do manage to learn it, it is almost impossible to make it look remotely elegant. Not that I'm trying to put you off or anything.

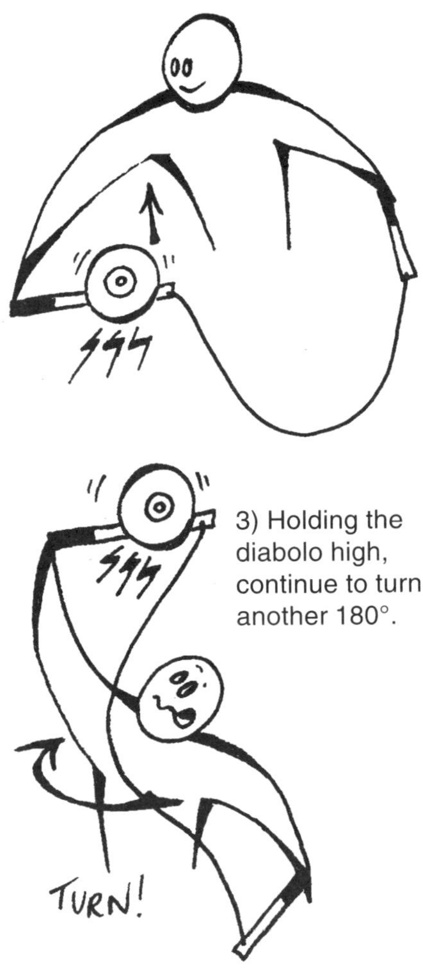

1) Carry the grind under your arm, then begin to lift it.

2) As you lift it, turn round 180°.

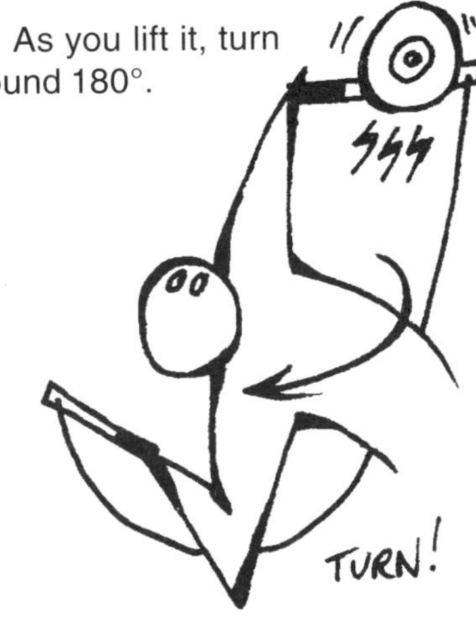

3) Holding the diabolo high, continue to turn another 180°.

4) Bring the diabolo back down to the starting position.

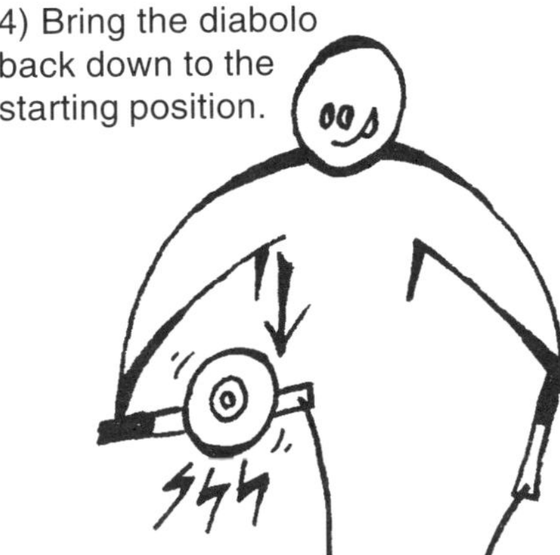

BIG HINT: So long as you have sufficient spin, allowing the diabolo to brush against your hand will help your control slightly.

Oh, and if you're really interested:
i) Reverse curls are possible too.
ii) Simultaneous curls with two diabolos aren't!

BUTTERFLY GRIND

They say that imitation is the sincerest form of flattery? Whatever. This move has been pilfered from the contact juggling fraternity. Personally, I think it looks better with a ball, but it *is* about ten times harder with a diabolo. That's got to be reason enough to learn it, eh?

The trick in essence consists of going from an inward grind to an outward grind by rolling the diabolo over the tip of the handstick.

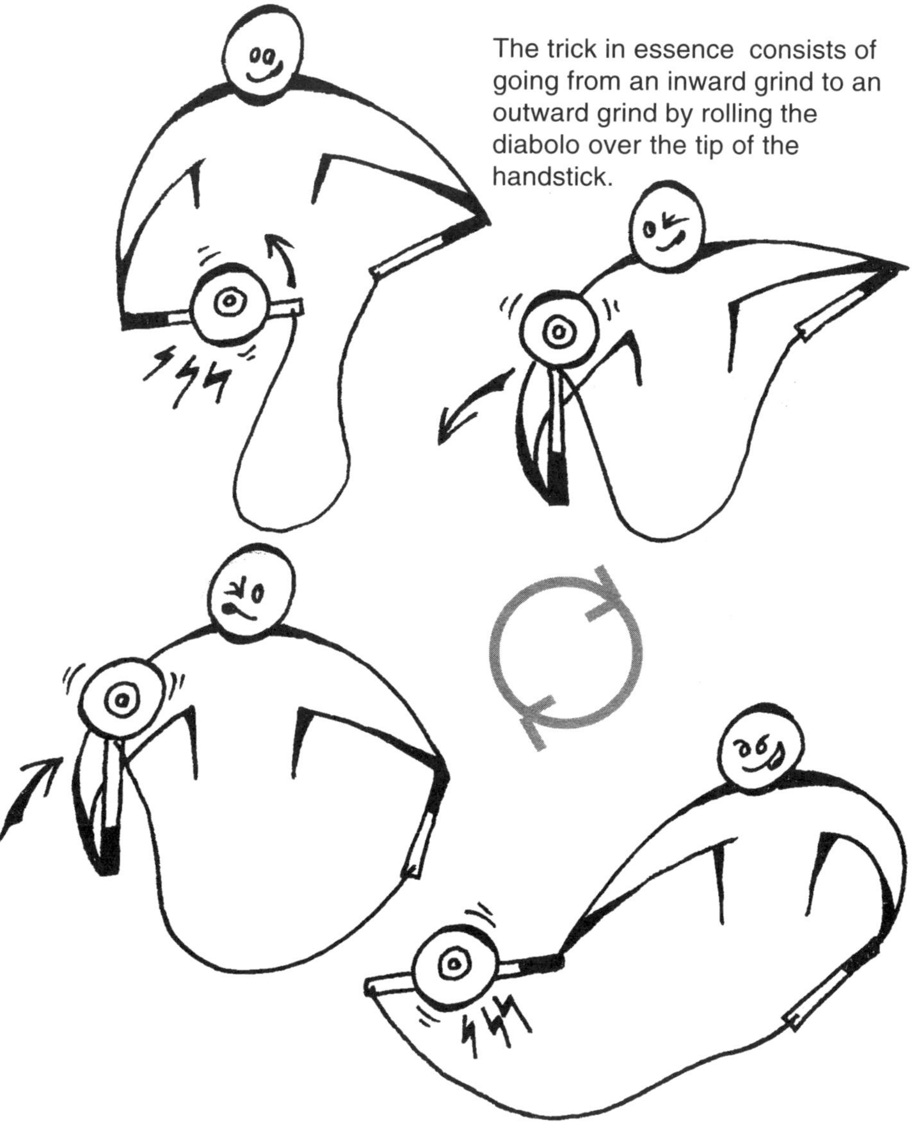

"Oh! Is THAT all?", I hear you cry (sarcastic swines!) Well, to make it easier, follow this progression:

1) Learn inward and outward grinds on the same stick (obviously).

2) Practice transferring between the two positions, firstly by throwing the diabolo (no higher than about six inches above the tip of the stick.)

3) Reduce the height of the throw - until, eventually, the diabolo doesn't actually leave contact at all, it simply rolls over the tip of the stick.

This trick can be performed in a couple of different styles:

i) Trying to keep the diabolo in the same place whilst moving your hand and stick.

ii) Keeping your hand stationary whilst moving the stick and diabolo from side to side.

Personally, I prefer the second version, but then, who am I to judge? Make up your own minds (I'm sure you probably would have anyway!)

STICK SWITCH GRIND BEHIND

This is very much a performance-worthy grind. Fortunately for you lot, if you can already stick switch grind and grind behind, then it really won't take that much effort to get the hang of it.

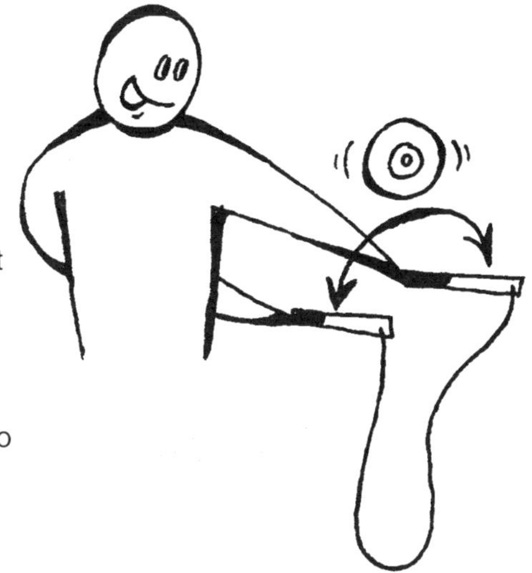

1) Get into an outward grind on your left handstick.

2) Bring your right hand tight around behind your back (so that you can see the stick).

3) Throw the diabolo from stick to stick.

Now learn it on the *right* side of your body, with your *left* hand behind your back.

Then try switching from behind the back on one side to behind the back on the other.

HAIR GRIND

If you haven't got long hair, you can always perform this on a hair wrap instead. If you haven't got *any* hair, then I'm afraid this will be a bit of a blunt pencil. Pointless.

1) Prepare your ~~victim~~ volunteer, making sure their
wrap/ plait is nice and tight. (Loose hair works fine
but the hair-plucking tangles caused by a spinning diabolo
can be truly nasty).
2) Throw the diabolo onto it.
3) They can then pop it back to you.

I know it's not exactly a show-stopper, but it *is* unusual enough (especially when done on your own hair!) to provide one of those stupid, surreal moments which no routine deserves to be without.

PRESSURE SUICIDE

Does it all get too much for you sometimes? Do you find it too hard to cope with pressure? Well, with this trick, you can let the pressure do the work for a change ...

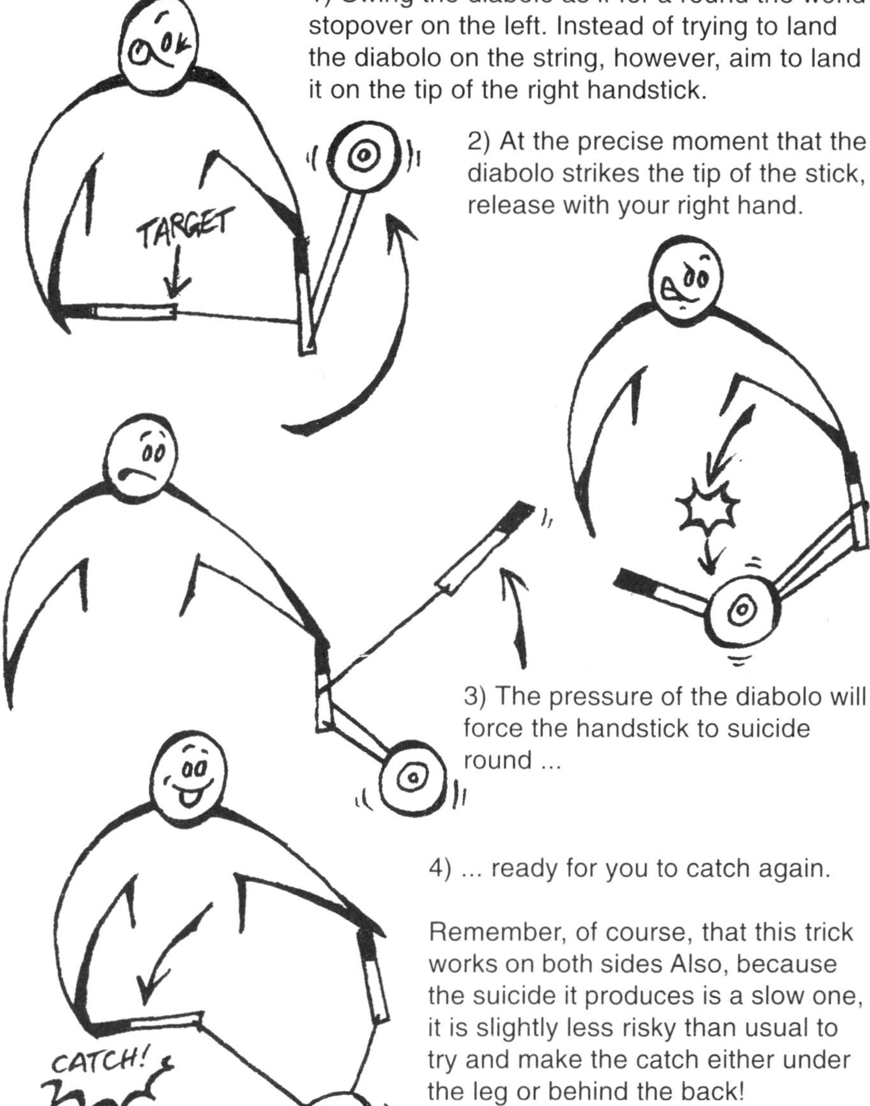

1) Swing the diabolo as if for a round the world stopover on the left. Instead of trying to land the diabolo on the string, however, aim to land it on the tip of the right handstick.

2) At the precise moment that the diabolo strikes the tip of the stick, release with your right hand.

3) The pressure of the diabolo will force the handstick to suicide round ...

4) ... ready for you to catch again.

Remember, of course, that this trick works on both sides Also, because the suicide it produces is a slow one, it is slightly less risky than usual to try and make the catch either under the leg or behind the back!
Grace under pressure, for sure.

OVERCIDE

This trick really *shouldn't* work. It just defies reality; I can *do* it consistently yet I still have no earthly idea *how* it works. In cases such as this, I fear it is best simply to accept rather than to question.

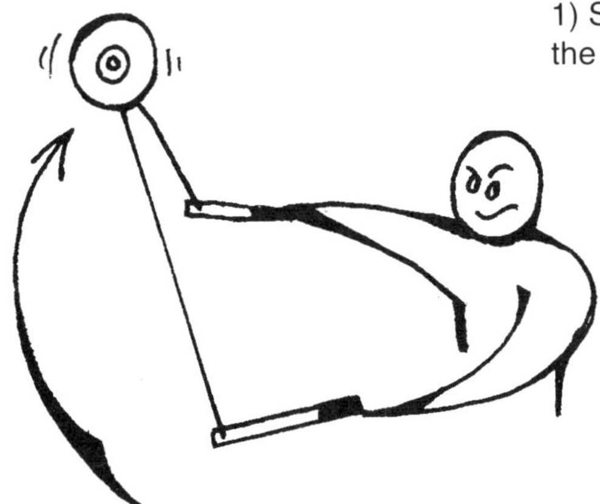

1) Swing an around the world to the right.

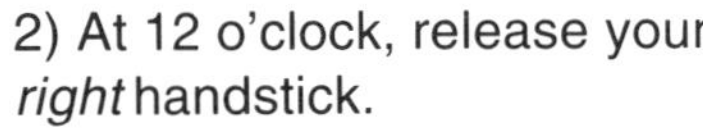

2) At 12 o'clock, release your *right* handstick.

3) As the diabolo comes around,
the handstick should swing in
underneath it.

4) Catch the stick. Pull tight. The
diabolo will climb the string.
Somehow.

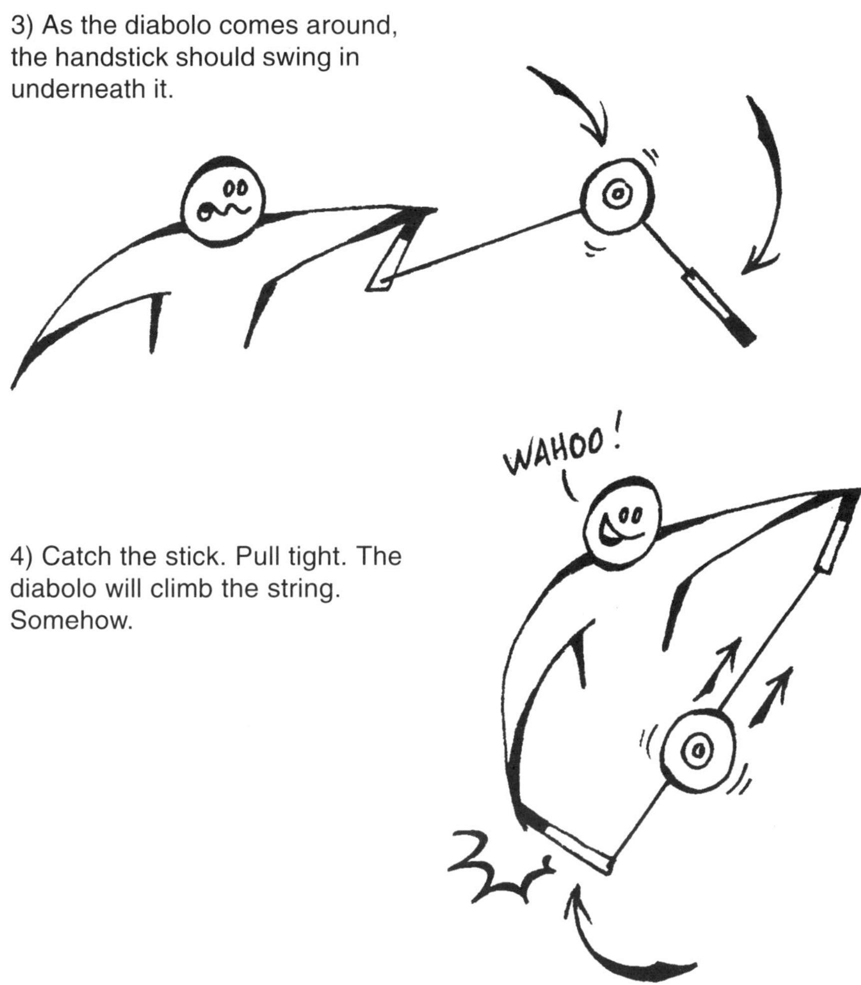

After the climb you will be left with a twisted string, which you can
dispose of with a round the world to the left.

BE CAREFUL, by the way, as the stick can come flying in at truly
knuckle-splintering speeds. Just thought you'd like to know.

SUICIDE LEAP

If you have sore kneecaps, I wouldn't recommend you try this trick. If you don't have sore knees, however, I'm sure you will soon.

1) Swing the diabolo to the right.

2) As you swing the diabolo back to the left, jump over the top of it.

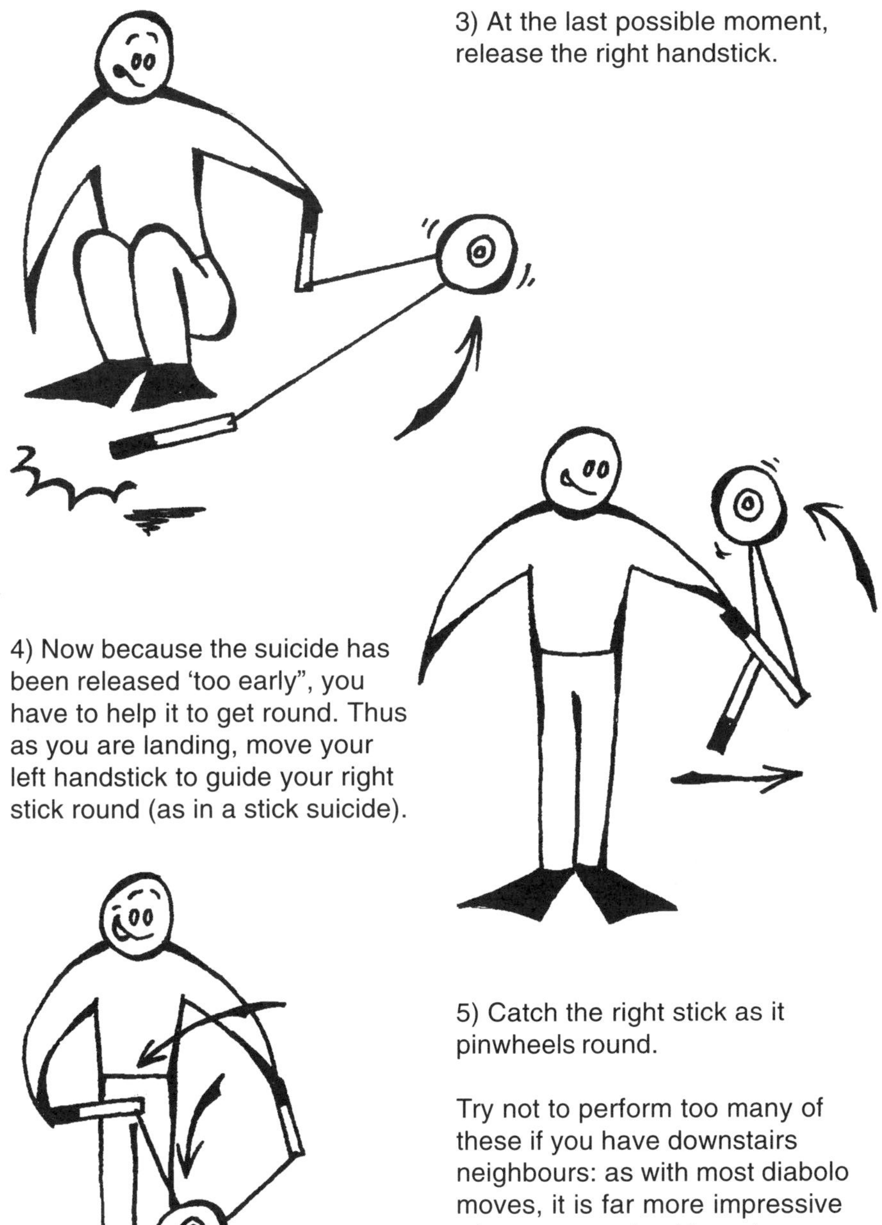

3) At the last possible moment, release the right handstick.

4) Now because the suicide has been released 'too early", you have to help it to get round. Thus as you are landing, move your left handstick to guide your right stick round (as in a stick suicide).

5) Catch the right stick as it pinwheels round.

Try not to perform too many of these if you have downstairs neighbours: as with most diabolo moves, it is far more impressive when seen and not heard.

PIROUETTE SUICIDE

Surely one of the most ridiculous suicide variations around. Make sure your audience knows just how difficult this is before performing it.

1) Swing and release a high, slow suicide.

2) As the diabolo passes 12 o'clock, perform a swift pirouette, making sure that you hold your left hand above your head so that you don't get tangled up.

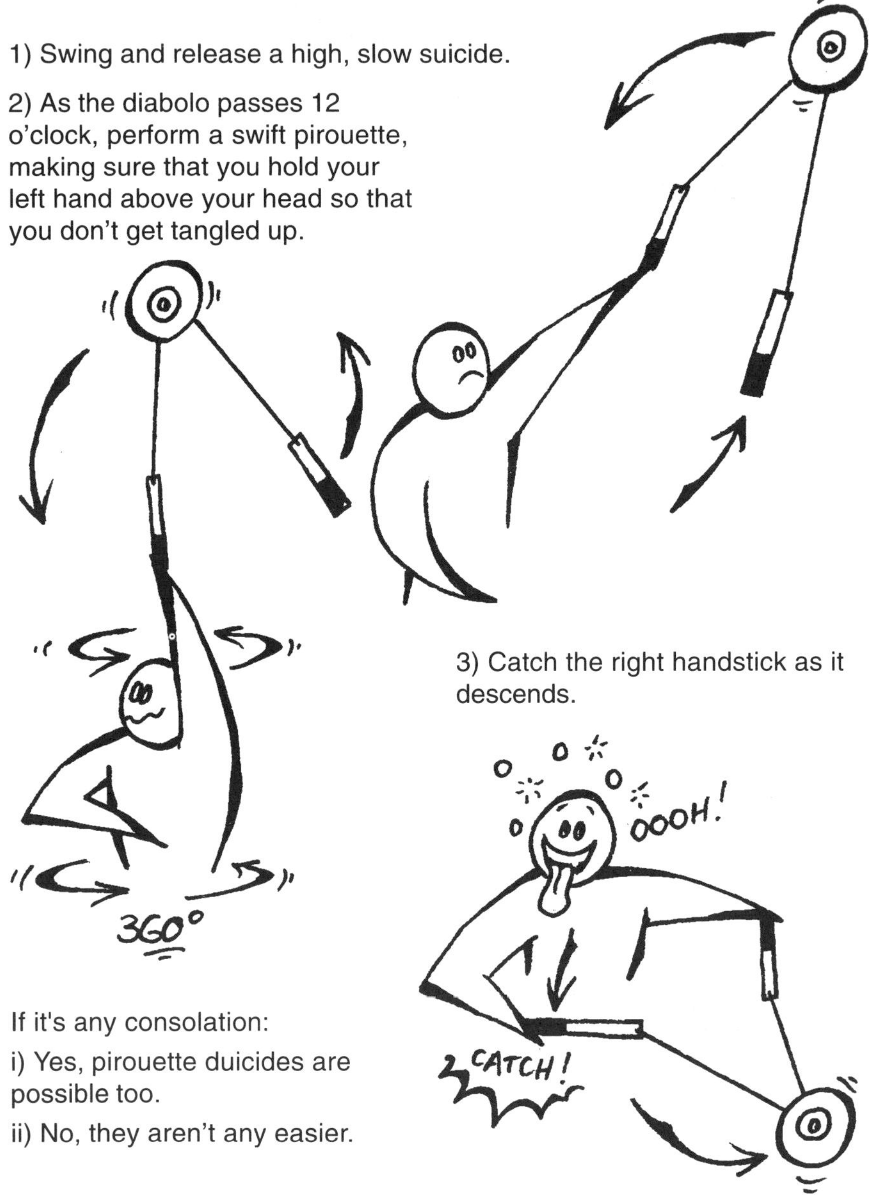

3) Catch the right handstick as it descends.

If it's any consolation:

i) Yes, pirouette duicides are possible too.

ii) No, they aren't any easier.

FLIPCIDE

A bizarre new suicide where the diabolo actually leaves the string half way through! No, I didn't believe it at first, either ...

1) Start with arms crossed, left over right.

2) Pull straight up with your left, and release the right stick as you pull. (It's vital that you pull straight up, not to the side, ok?)

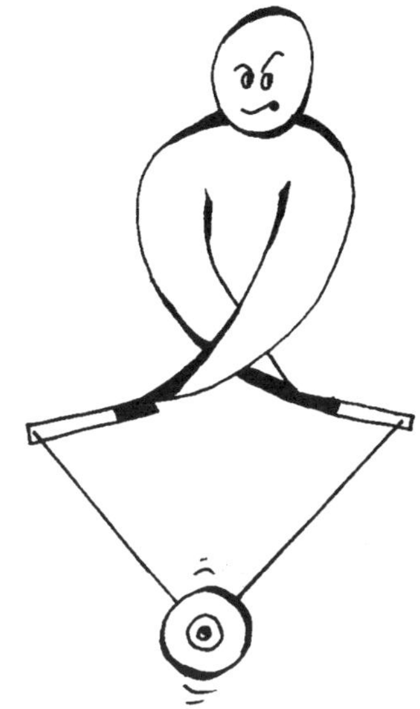

3) The diabolo will leave the string and the handstick will swing right round.

4) Catch the string, and slide your hand down to the stick.

5) Now catch the diabolo.

High ceilings help with this one. So does a shorter string. An unrelenting belief in the apparently impossible would probably help too.

It can't get any worse ...

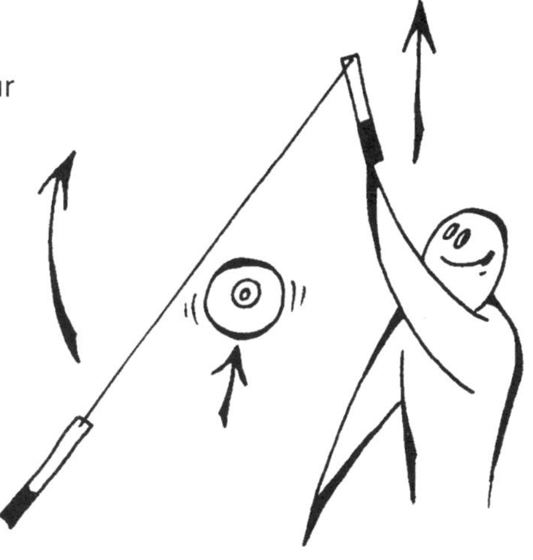

GENOCIDE

Ok, it *can* get worse.

If any one trick sums up how much the diabolo has progressed in the past few years then this is it. Forget the humble suicide. Forget whip catches. Forget milking the cow (good idea ...) This is PURE AND SIMPLE LUNACY.

Originally titled the "downcide", I felt that such a name failed to sum up the sheer insanity of this manouevre. This trick will not only turn the heads of anyone nearby, it will probably remove them too. It's DANGEROUS, so please be careful.

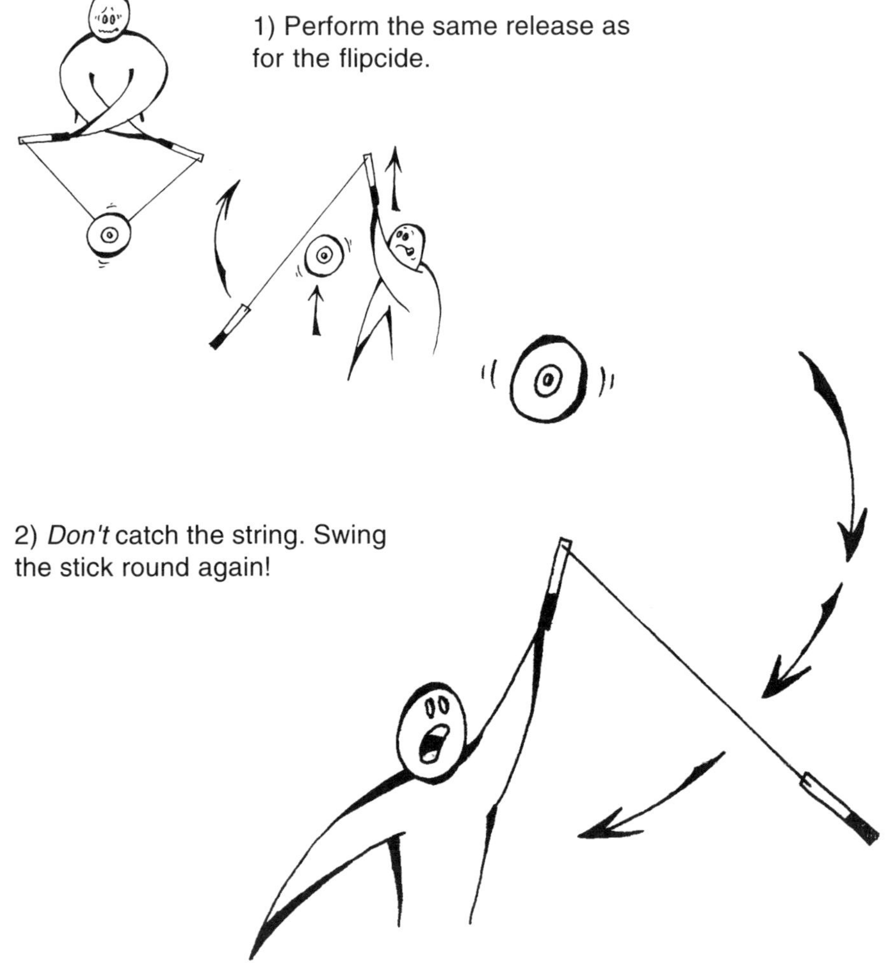

1) Perform the same release as for the flipcide.

2) *Don't* catch the string. Swing the stick round again!

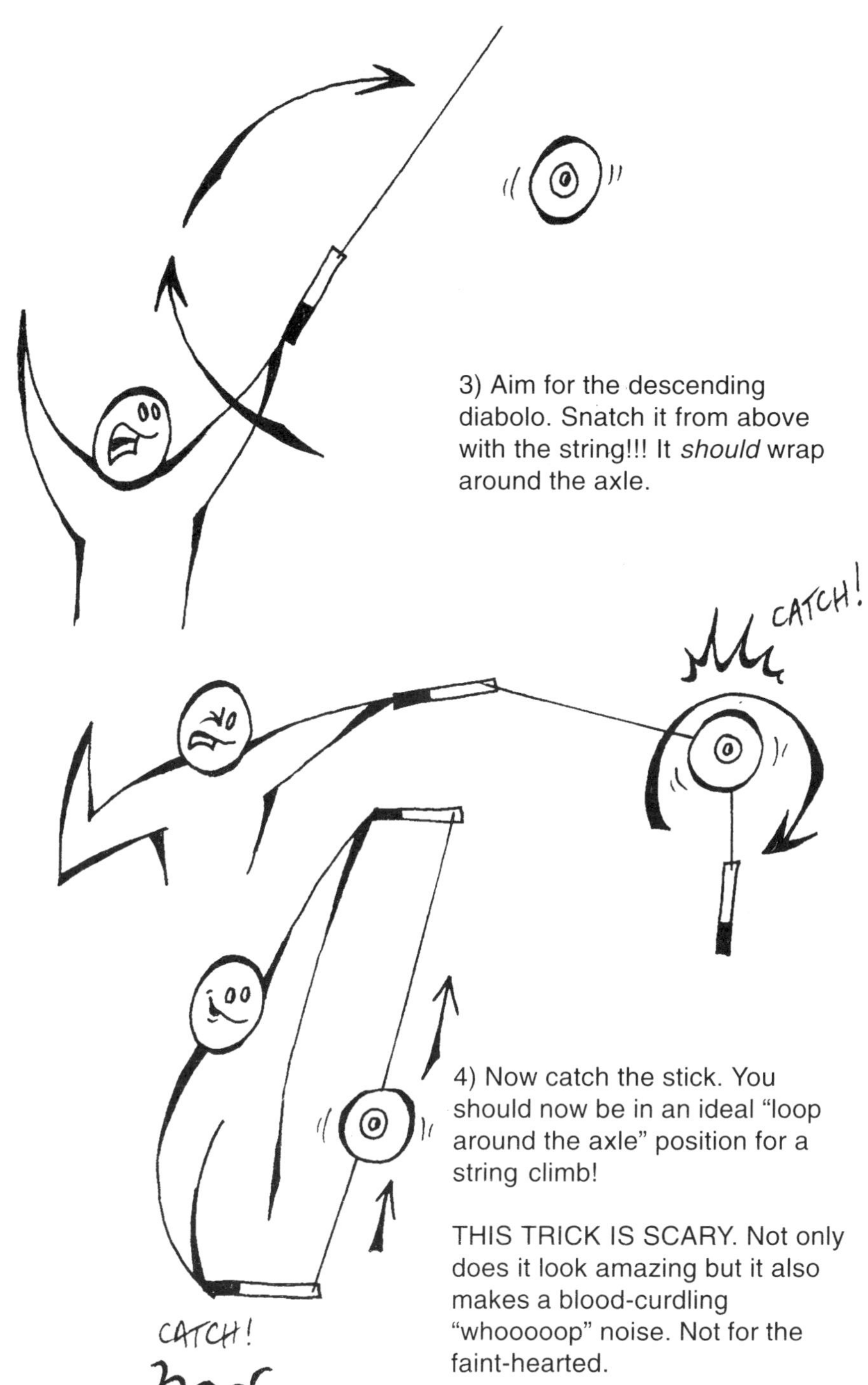

3) Aim for the descending diabolo. Snatch it from above with the string!!! It *should* wrap around the axle.

4) Now catch the stick. You should now be in an ideal "loop around the axle" position for a string climb!

THIS TRICK IS SCARY. Not only does it look amazing but it also makes a blood-curdling "whoooooop" noise. Not for the faint-hearted.

HOMICIDE

The subtle art of removing objects from people's mouths with the stick during a suicide. Success leads to praise, applause and stardom. Failure? Well, Let's just say the trick is aptly named ...
Want to learn it? Here are a few words of wisdom (and warning).
1) If you're *really* scared of this trick, practice hitting things which are hanging over the edge of shelves. Get your eye in, right?
2) Once you move onto live targets, learn with something *long* first. Stick a couple of straws together, perhaps.
3) Make sure your victim is holding the target in their *lips* (preferably moistened), *not* their teeth.
4) Aim for the tip, *not* the middle.

Eventually you should be able to take out a cigarette. (If people are worried about their health, use a toothbrush. Or a toothpick (???) Then you can learn it with two diabolos. The best I ever managed (somewhat foolishly) was to take a razor out of someone's mouth with a two diabolo suicide.
Oh, and just in case anything goes wrong ... practice apologising as sincerely and profusely as possible.

AROUND THE KNEE

The actual skill for this trick is, of course, no different to that for around the leg. The difficult part is managing to stand still on one leg while doing it. So basically the instructions for this trick read roughly as follows:

1) Learn to stand in this position.

2) Learn to diabolo in this position.

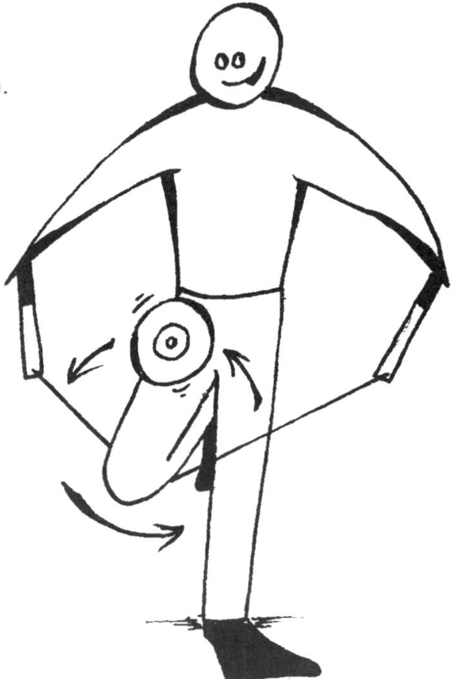

If you have trouble with the second part, never mind - maybe you can get a job as a stork or something.

ARM SCOOP (NO 3)

Yet another arm scoop trick, but this one is especially handy as, unlike the others, it can be performed in the *middle* of an around the arm sequence. Read on for true enlightenment.

1) Pop the diabolo two or three inches into the air. This time scoop *down* on it with your *right* hand.

2) Lift the diabolo over with your right hand.

3) And allow it to roll back under your arm into the starting position.

A few around the arms, followed by a few of these, then one of the previous arm scoops to finish should be enough to convince most audiences that you are indeed a God. Or at least a very talented waster.

RUBBERWRIST SCOOP

The filthiest little round the arm trick that I've ever had the misfortune to come across. It's awkward, hurts a bit and looks truly bizarre. These, as you are painfully aware by now, are three of the prime requisites for any trick getting into one of these books ...

1) Start in a normal around the right arm position.

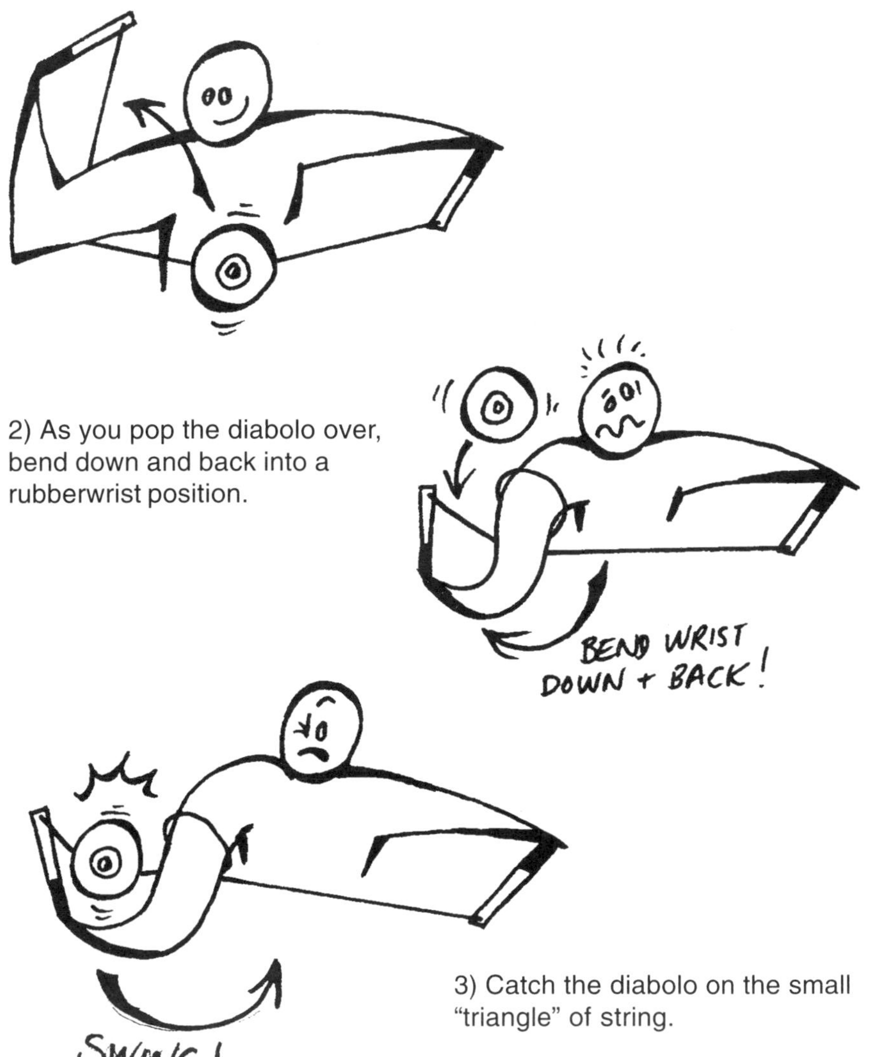

2) As you pop the diabolo over, bend down and back into a rubberwrist position.

3) Catch the diabolo on the small "triangle" of string.

4) Allow the diabolo to swing under your arm ...

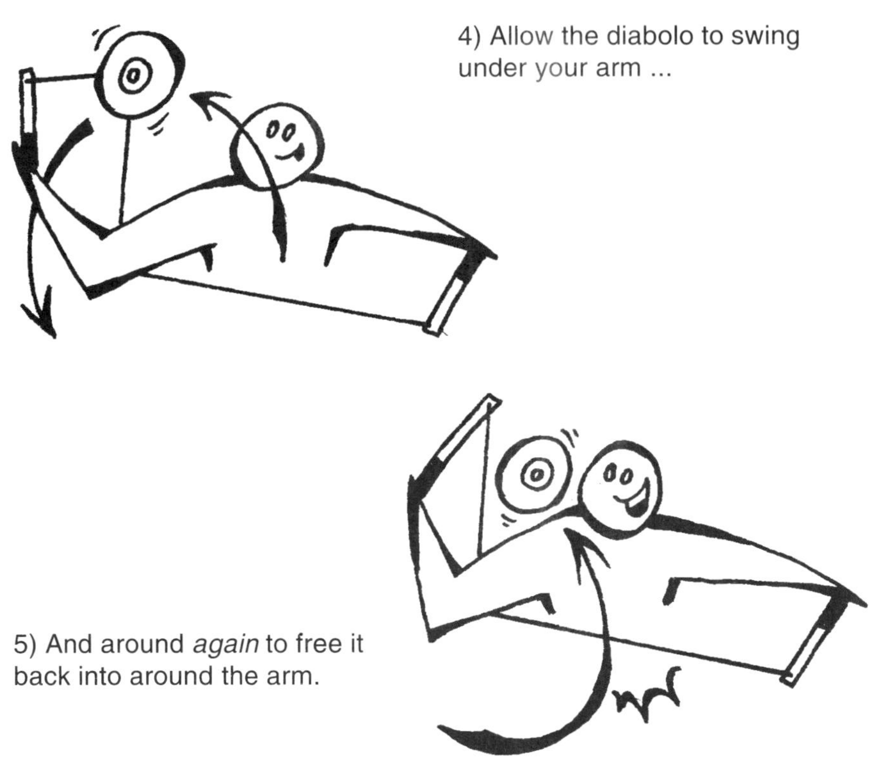

5) And around *again* to free it back into around the arm.

It's a good idea to practice this move with someone holding the diabolo for you at first. It *is* complicated, but 100% worth it for the mysterious "twice around the limb" visual effect it produces.

RICOCHETS

Ricochets are basically very fast bounces from side to side across any particular part of the body you wish. I've shown the most basic one, across the foot, in full. Once you've got the hang of one, the others should follow fairly quickly.

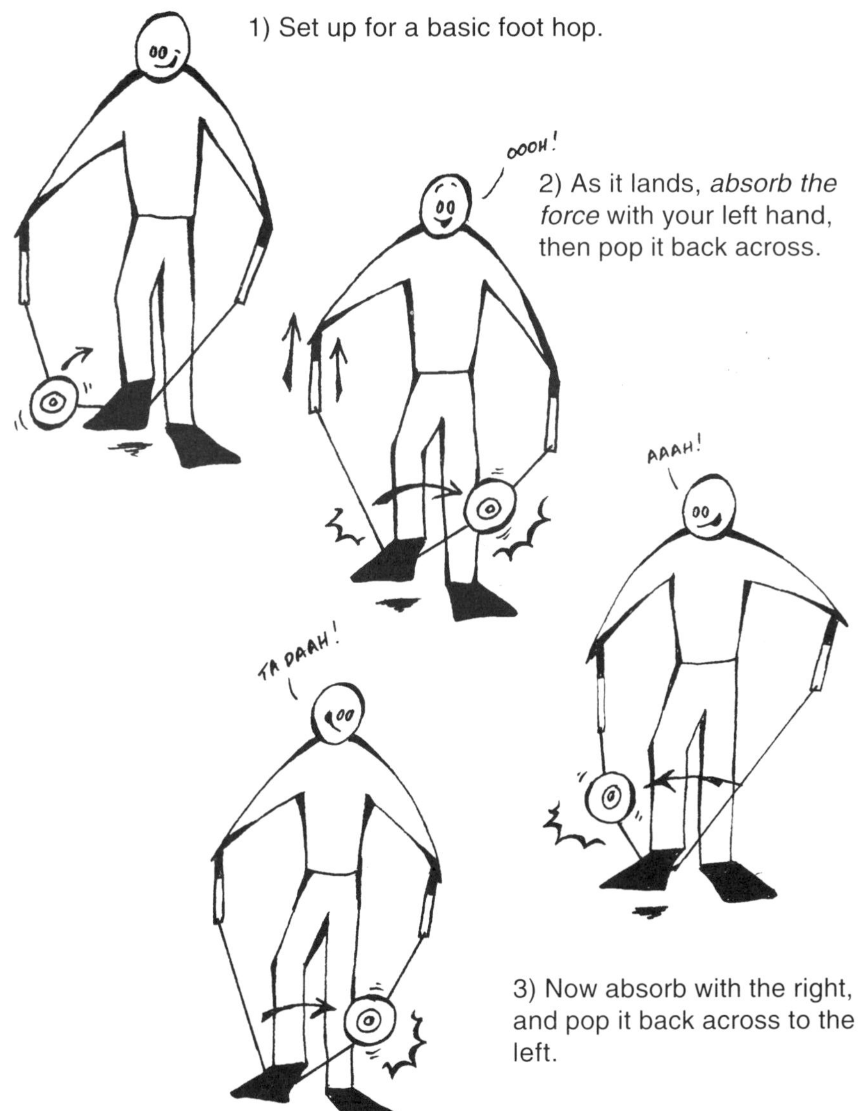

1) Set up for a basic foot hop.

2) As it lands, *absorb the force* with your left hand, then pop it back across.

3) Now absorb with the right, and pop it back across to the left.

At first, this will be a very slow trick, but with practice it is possible to make the diabolo ricochet back and forth with alarming ferocity. If you find the foot too easy, why not try these variations:

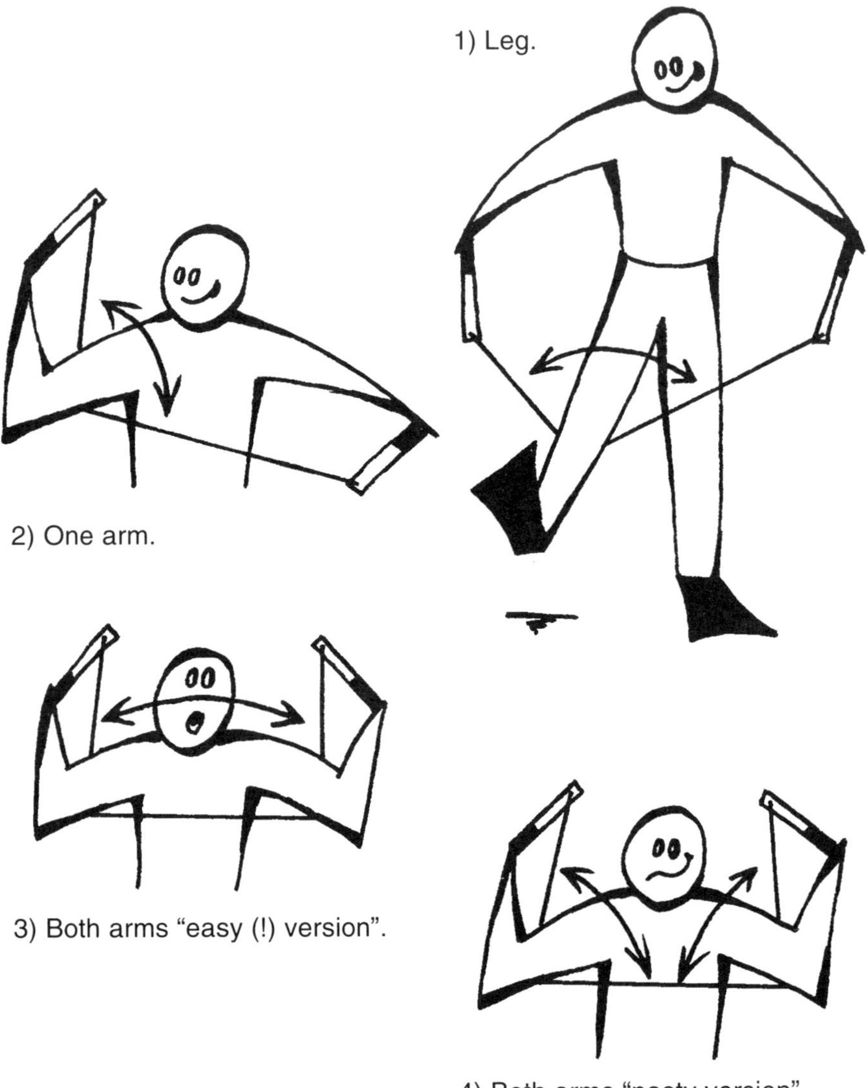

1) Leg.

2) One arm.

3) Both arms "easy (!) version".

4) Both arms "nasty version".

FIGURE 8 AROUND BOTH LEGS

There is a hard way to do this, and an easy way to do this. In my all encompassing ignorance, I did it the hard way for over a year before realising that the easy way existed. Story of my life, really.

1) Face to your right. Get the diabolo circling around your left leg.

2) Now reach behind your back with your left stick to pop the diabolo over your right leg. (It is important to watch the diabolo carefully as this throw is performed blind.)

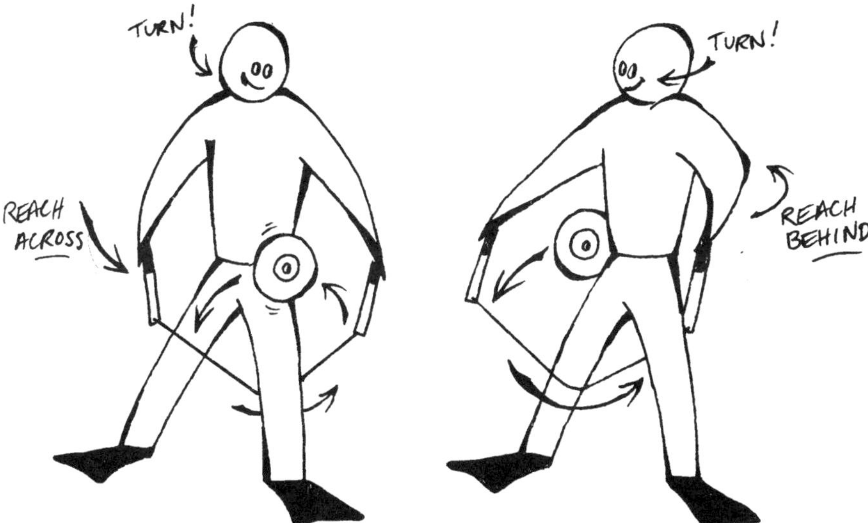

In time, you should be able to circle comfortably around either leg, and also alternate (left, right, left, right), swaying your upper body gently from side to side.

Just in case you hadn't already guessed, the harder version involves facing to your left before starting. Wow, you may notice, the *catch* behind your left leg is now blind. Not easy. But possible. I should know.

RUBBERWRIST BOUNCE

If you find rubberwrist catches awkward or painful, I wholeheartedly advise that you ignore this trick completely.

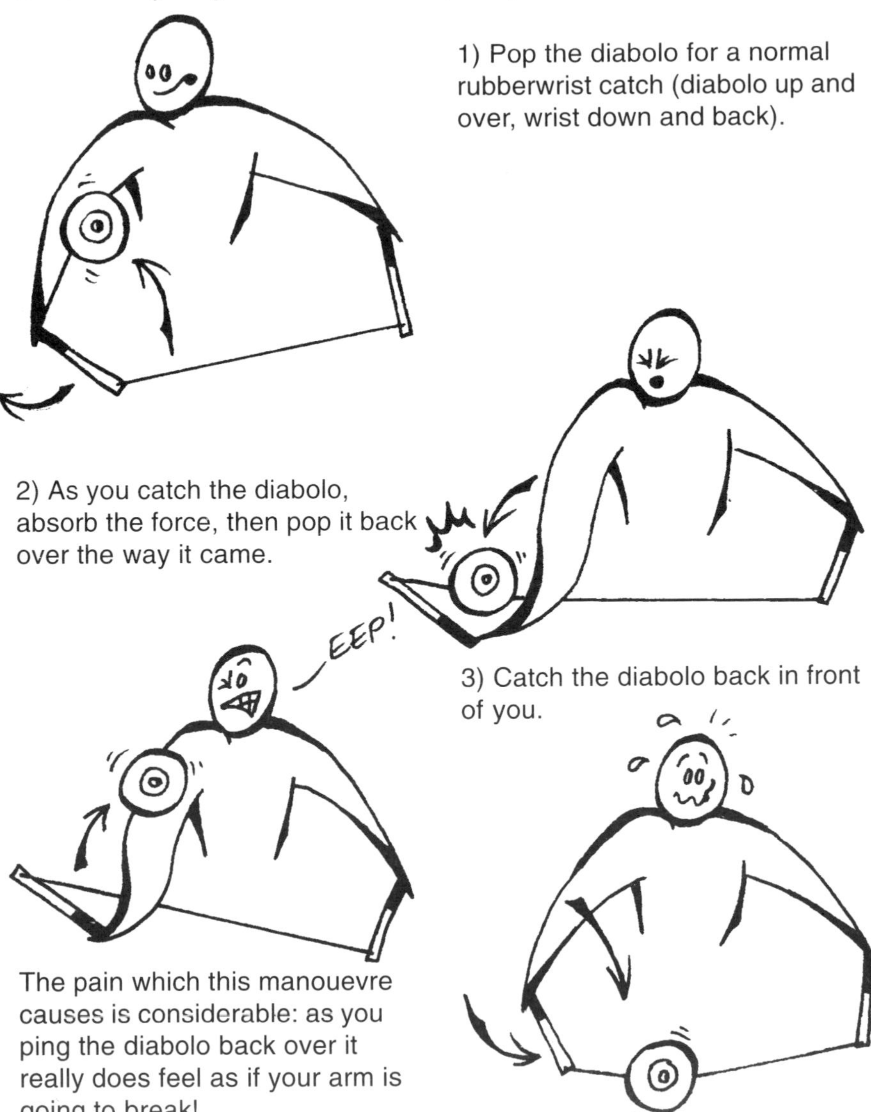

1) Pop the diabolo for a normal rubberwrist catch (diabolo up and over, wrist down and back).

2) As you catch the diabolo, absorb the force, then pop it back over the way it came.

3) Catch the diabolo back in front of you.

The pain which this manouevre causes is considerable: as you ping the diabolo back over it really does feel as if your arm is going to break!

If this isn't enough for the masochists amongst you, why not try 'rubberwrist tennis", bouncing all the way from your left side to your right. Ah! The sweet, sweet suffering.

CROSS ARM TRAPS

This trick has a similar arm movement to the classic 3-ball trick "Mills' Mess". Unfortunately, it lacks most of the grace and finesse of the Mess, but it still looks fairly impressive. Beauty is in the eye of the beholder, is it not?

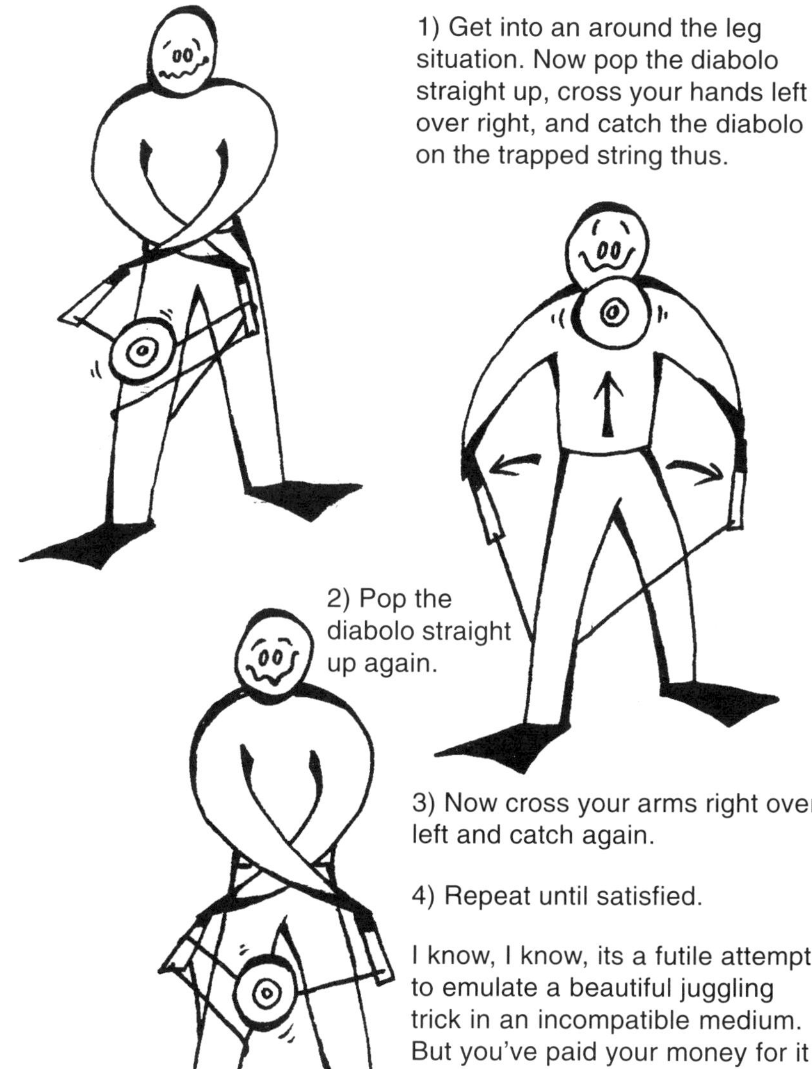

1) Get into an around the leg situation. Now pop the diabolo straight up, cross your hands left over right, and catch the diabolo on the trapped string thus.

2) Pop the diabolo straight up again.

3) Now cross your arms right over left and catch again.

4) Repeat until satisfied.

I know, I know, its a futile attempt to emulate a beautiful juggling trick in an incompatible medium. But you've paid your money for it now, so you might as well learn it.

ARM STOPOVER SCOOP

If you take time to look at this one carefully, you will realise that it is in fact a subtle fusion of two separate moves. But when put together smoothly, they produce this unusually fast, direction-changing-tangling-up sort of trick. Your audience won't know what hit them.

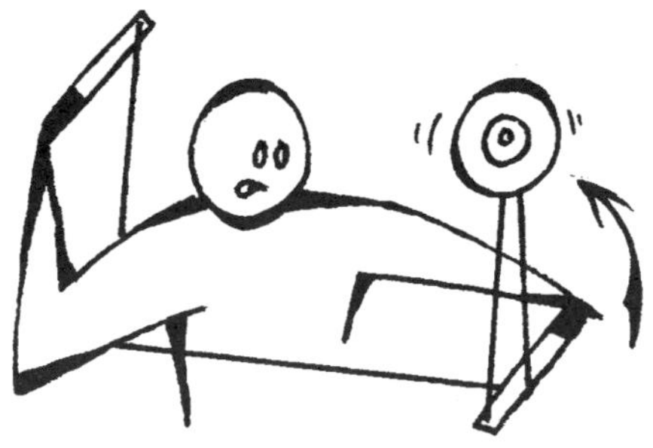

1) Get the diabolo going around your right arm. Now *without* coming out of the arm position, perform a stopover on the left handstick.

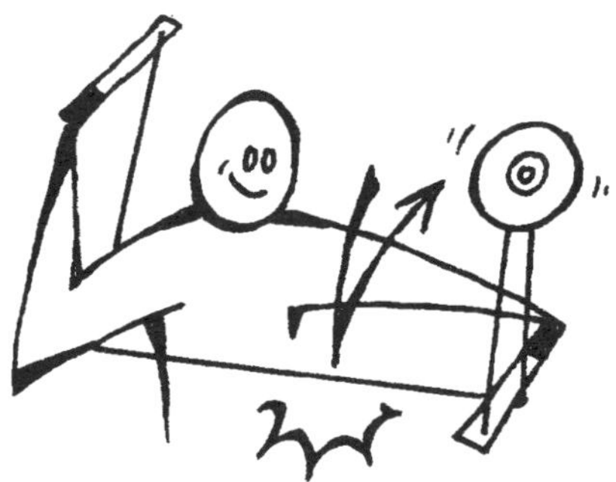

2) Quickly bounce the diabolo out of the stopover.

3) As the diabolo comes back around, lower your right hand ...

4) ... and nimbly perform a normal arm scoop.

5) The diabolo will, as usual, come around so that you can throw to escape with arms crossed, right over left.

Fluidity is the secret of this one, otherwise it just looks like two separate moves. With practice the diabolo should follow a smooth, S-shaped curve. (Yes, I know ... I said the "p" word again!)

ARM KICKBACK

Rather a simple one this, but that doesn't mean that it isn't impressive. A longer string makes this one slightly easier, but don't any of you "shorties' *dare* use it as an excuse, ok?

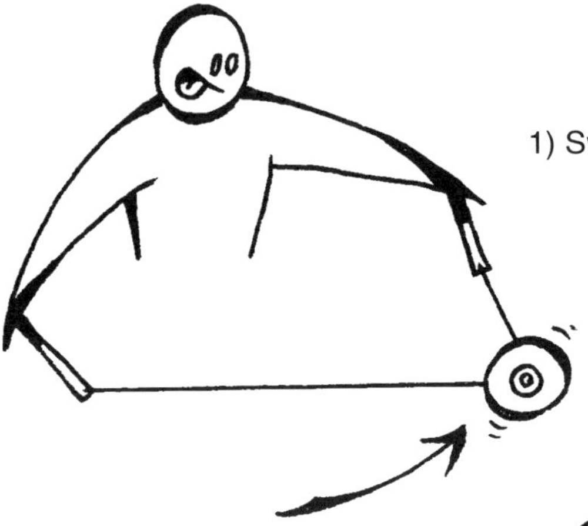

1) Swing for an around the world.

2) Instead of passing between your arms as usual, the diabolo swings over your right upper arm.

3) As it swings round, keep your right forearm erect and your left arm as straight as your string will allow.

4) Let the diabolo bounce off the
underside of the string near your
left handstick.

5) And let it swing back over,
untangled, from whence it came.

The trickiest bit of the whole procedure is the actual bounce, but with
practice it shouldn't present any real difficulties. I know I said it was
simple, but I didn't say anything about it being easy, did I?

ARM STALL

A truly elegant move which also looks particularly flashy when used to catch a high throw.

1) When the diabolo is up in the air, cock your right wrist and lay the string tight on top of your arm.

2) Catch the diabolo over your arm.

3) Now lift the diabolo over by swinging an around the world to the left.

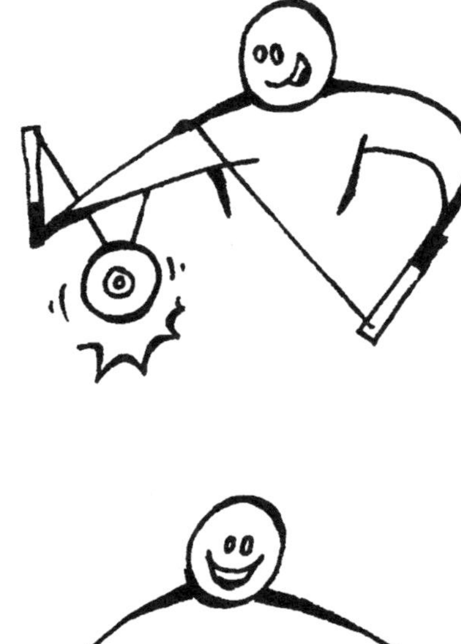

And yes, I *know* it feels harder to do on the other side, but just learn it, ok? Nobody said you were here to enjoy yourself, did they?

UNDER LEG SCOOP

Essentially, this is the same as an unwrap and recapture,
but *do not be deceived* - the insertion of the limb
makes the final throw *much* harder.

1) Unwrap on the right hand side
while lifting your leg.

2) As the diabolo swings under
your leg:
i) Reach under your leg with your
right stick.
ii) Reach *across* your body with
your left stick.
And throw.

Learn this trick on both sides *and*
under both legs. Once this
becomes too easy, why not try
and explore the realms of albert/
trebla scoops as well?

SCOOP BEHIND

Again, this is basically an unwrap and recapture, but this time the "insertion" of the whole body makes it even more difficult to master.

1) Unwrap on the right, stepping forwards as you do so.

2) Reach *across* with your left and *behind* with your right.

Throw the diabolo up over your left shoulder. (This should all occur as one fluid movement!)

Repetition of this move in a left-right-left manner produces a motion similar to that of back crosses in "normal" juggling. The level of difficulty, unfortunately, is comparable too.

AROUND BOTH ARMS (FIGURE 8 REVERSE)

At first glance, this looks exactly the same as the "Around Both Arms figure of 8" in *Diabolo 2*. Look closer, however, and you will see that the arrows go in the *opposite* direction.

This means that the throws are now made from the *outsides* and the catches occur in the middle.

This actually makes this an easier variation, although no less impressive to the untrained eye. If you want to, try starting with one version, then switch into the other.

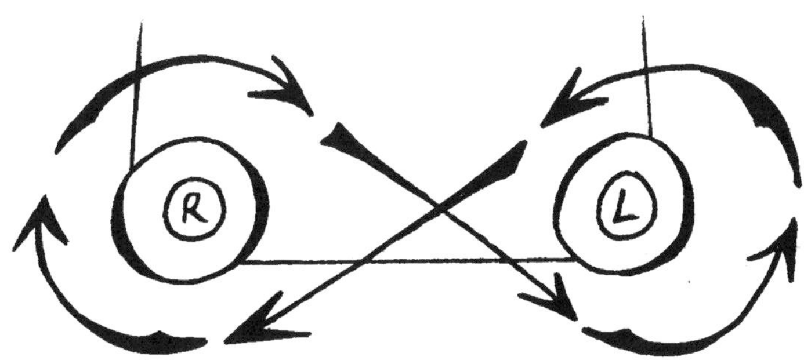

Thanks to a certain Mr B Brolly for pointing this one out!

AROUND CROSSED ARMS

If you aren't partial to "around both arms" tricks, then pretend that you didn't see this page. If, however, you *did* struggle valiantly through all the "both arm" variations, then welcome to them all again ... this time with your arms crossed!

1) Unwrap on the *right hand side*.

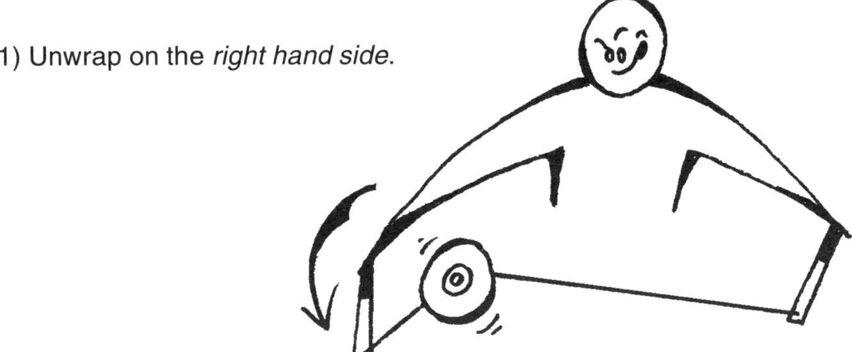

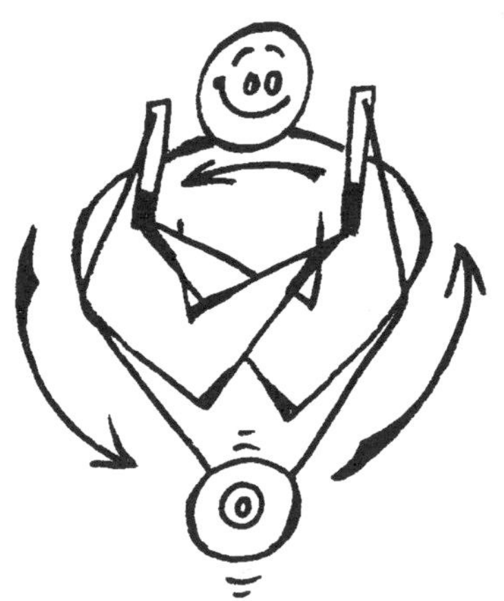

2) Cross your arms with the *left hand* nearest to you. Cross them at the *wrists*, not at the elbows. Now keep your upper arms horizontal, your wrists cocked slightly and positioned directly in front of your face. By moving both arms circularly in sync, it is possible to make the diabolo circle your arms. But, boy oh boy, it's awkward at first!

Once (if ever) you're used to this, try making the diabolo circle one arm, then the other.
Try figure 8's.
Try ricochets.
Try sticking your head in there as well.
Try getting a life, perchance?

UPWHIP

Bizarrely enough, whip catches *do* in fact work in both directions ...

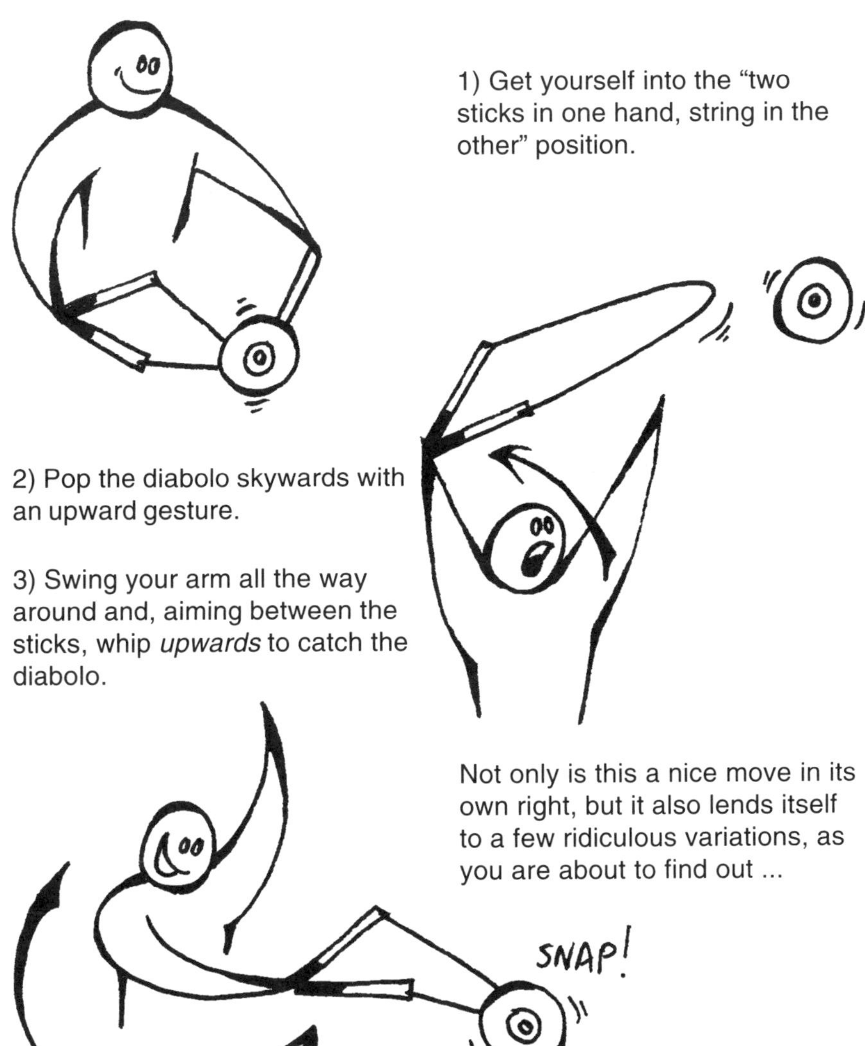

1) Get yourself into the "two sticks in one hand, string in the other" position.

2) Pop the diabolo skywards with an upward gesture.

3) Swing your arm all the way around and, aiming between the sticks, whip *upwards* to catch the diabolo.

Not only is this a nice move in its own right, but it also lends itself to a few ridiculous variations, as you are about to find out ...

TREBLA WHIP

Ooooh! Sounds just like a fancy pudding, doesn't it? Just be careful: get it wrong and you might end up with chopped nuts for extra topping.

1) Once again prepare for a whip, this time standing with your legs spread.

2) Pop the diabolo into the air and reach behind your back.

3) Now "just" perform an upwhip between your legs to snag the diabolo before it hits the floor. If this all sounds a "trifle" risky (oh dear, oh dear), why not plump for the next variation instead?

WHIP BEHIND

If ever there was a trick in the whole of juggling which oozes with style and positively drips with panache, then this is it. Unfortunately it is almost impossible to land every time, but when you are successful, it is guaranteed to melt the brains of everyone watching. This trick is suave, risky and totally sexy: land it once and I promise you all other tricks will never seem the same again.

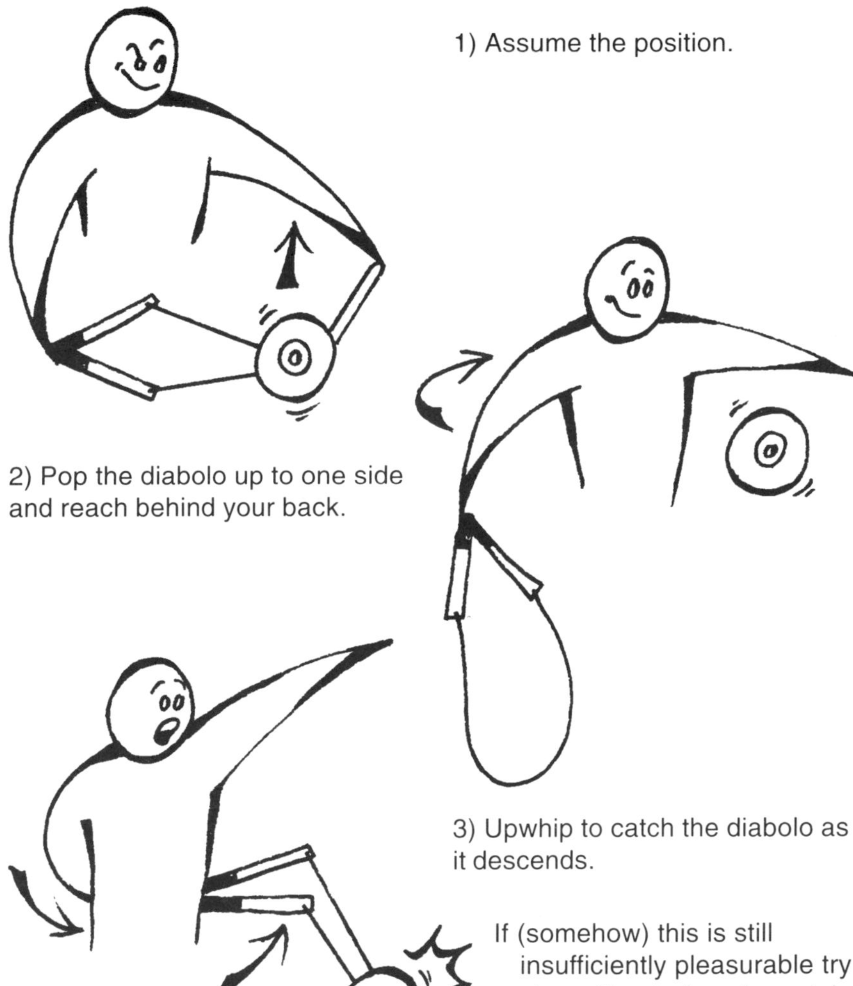

1) Assume the position.

2) Pop the diabolo up to one side and reach behind your back.

3) Upwhip to catch the diabolo as it descends.

If (somehow) this is still insufficiently pleasurable try pirouetting before the catch ... awesome is too small a word.

SHOULDER WHIP

Yet another whip catch. This one - when performed correctly - has an air of nonchalance which few others can surpass.

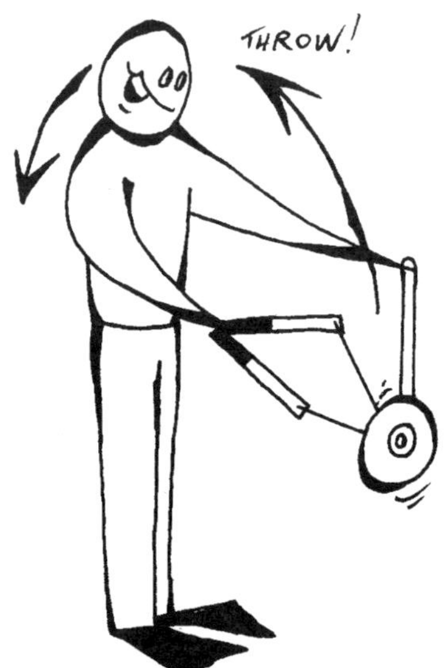

1) Set up in the usual "sticks in one hand, string in the other, face the diabolo" way.

2) Throw the diabolo over your right shoulder.

3) Whip over the right shoulder to catch the diabolo.

By fixing your gaze deliberately upon something straight ahead of you (see diagram!) this trick can be performed "blind". Especially effective if you use it as your last trick as you saunter smoothly off stage.

ALBERT WHIP

Okay, so the behind the back whip is the smoothest, sexiest whip catch, but *this* one is surely the ultimate. Contortion, ungainliness and total commitment to a blind catch all combine to give this trick the glorious title "nastiest bad bunch". Land it once then retire.

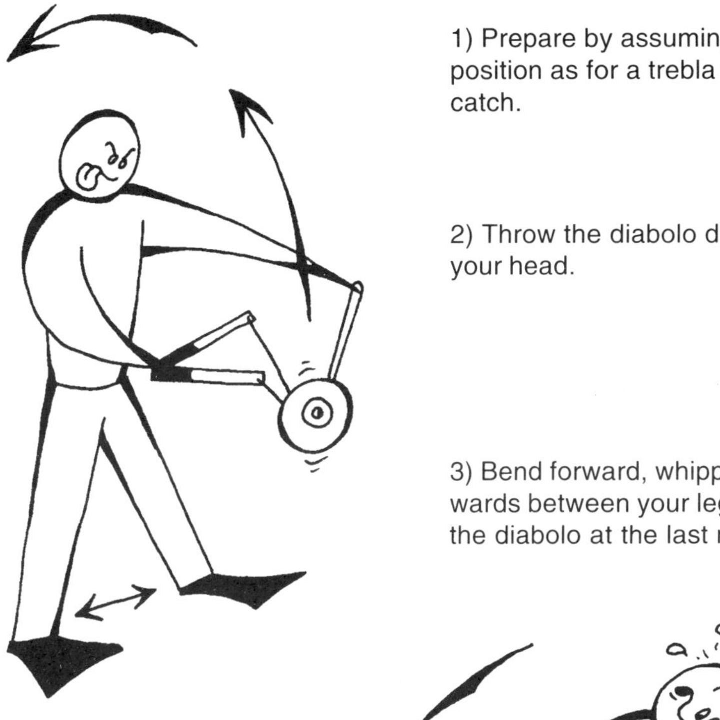

1) Prepare by assuming the same position as for a trebla whip catch.

2) Throw the diabolo directly over your head.

3) Bend forward, whipping upwards between your legs to catch the diabolo at the last minute!

This is the hardest version there is. I can't think of any more just yet. But don't ask me to come up with something worse. You know what I'm capable of ...

ALTERNATIVE FLOOR START

Ok, so this one *does* look ever so slightly less impressive than the other floor start. What it has got going for it however, is a far higher success rate. Surely that's what matters in the long run.

1) Set the diabolos up as shown. The tip of the right handstick pushes the left diabolo along as you roll everything to the left.

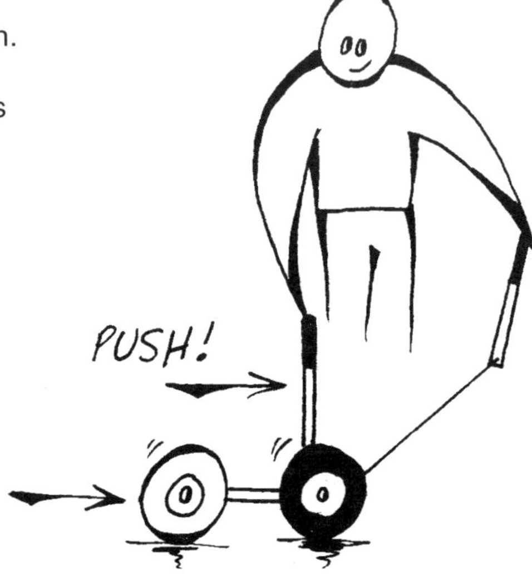

2) Lift up and start to shuffle. The diabolos still won't exactly be revolving at a rate of knots, but they will be spinning faster than they did in the old start. Small victories, my friends, small victories.

START OF DARKNESS

(apologies to Joseph Conrad)

If you want to open your two diabolo routine in spectacular fashion, then look no further. This is probably the hardest, nastiest start you will ever have the misfortune to come across.

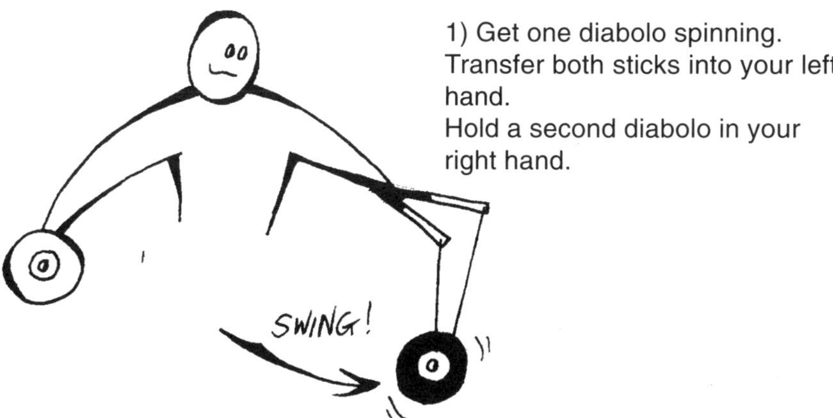

1) Get one diabolo spinning.
Transfer both sticks into your left hand.
Hold a second diabolo in your right hand.

2) Swing the spinning diabolo, releasing one stick into a suicide.

3) As it suicides round, hand launch the diabolo in your right hand. (Remember you can hand launch as high as you like, if you need more time.)

4) Catch the handstick.

5) Catch the descending diabolo into a shuffle.

If you find the "one handed suicide" difficult, practice it on its own until you can do it comfortably. No need to make this any harder than it already is, is there?

ROUND THE WORLD FEED

A slower round the world variation which occurs directly in front of the body, as opposed to slightly to the side with most others.

1) Swing for a normal round the world.

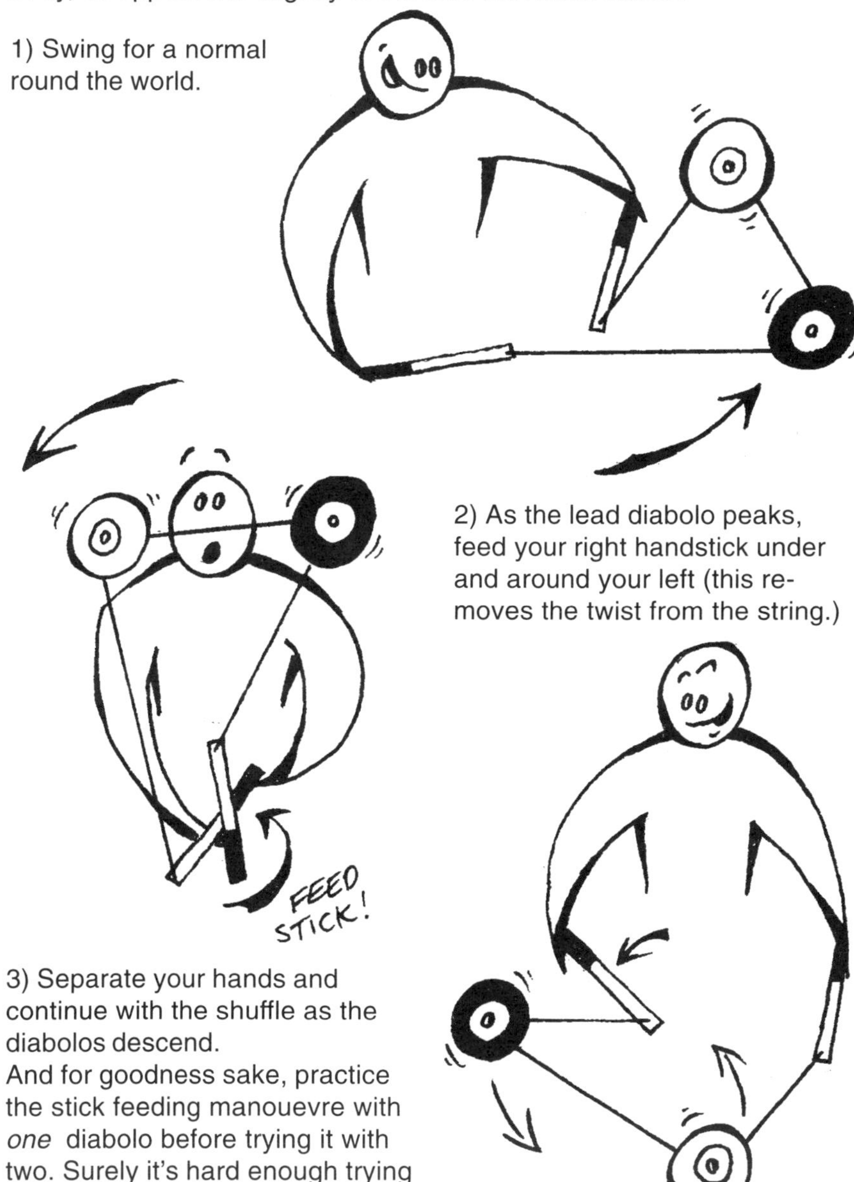

2) As the lead diabolo peaks, feed your right handstick under and around your left (this removes the twist from the string.)

3) Separate your hands and continue with the shuffle as the diabolos descend.

And for goodness sake, practice the stick feeding manouevre with *one* diabolo before trying it with two. Surely it's hard enough trying to learn one new move at a time?

STOPOVER BOTH SIDES

If one stopover simply wasn't enough for you ...

1) Perform a stopover on the left.

2) As you come out of the stopover, let the moving diabolo pass beneath its counterpart ...

3) ... and into a stopover on the left.

4) Come out of *this* stopover and you're back into the shuffle. Too easy? Then try substituting one (or even both) of the stopovers for a swing to overhead grind. Or even more bizarre, why not try the next trick?

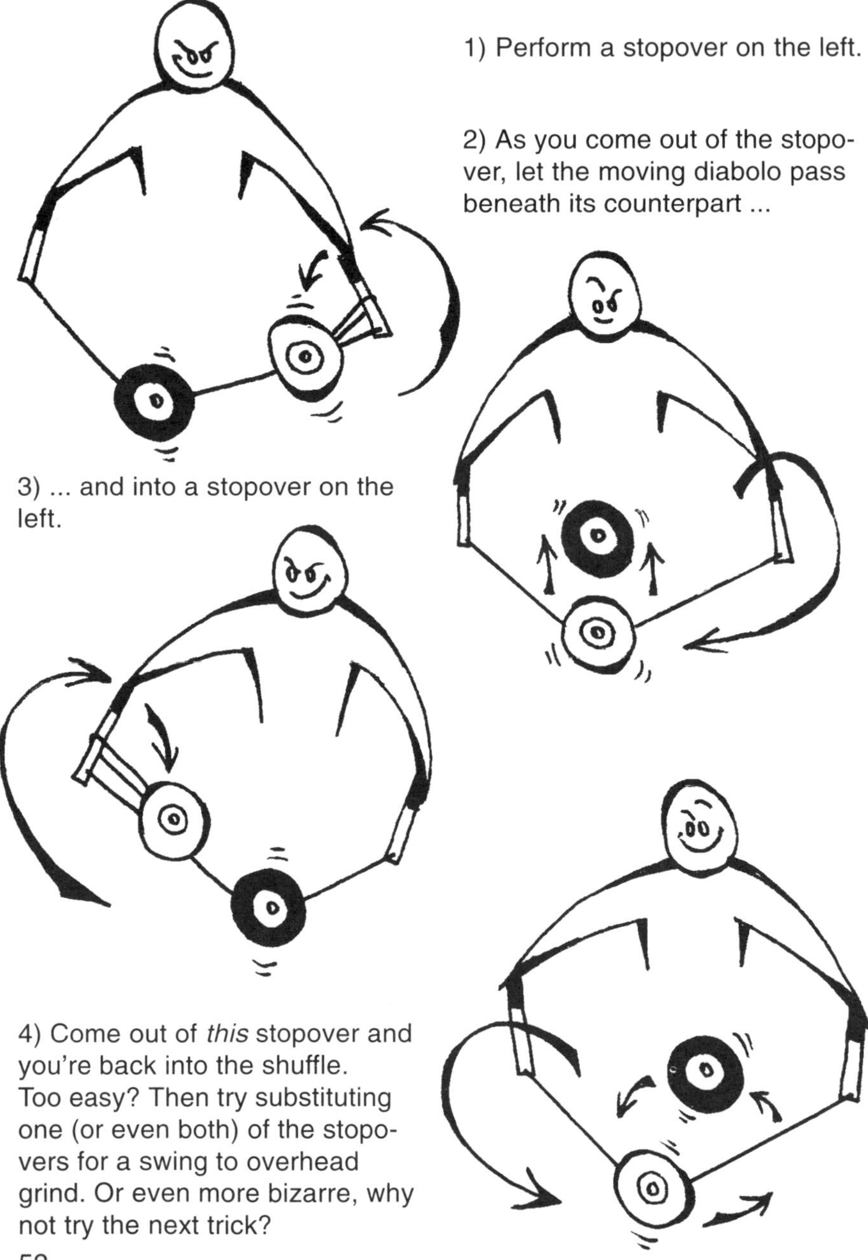

HYPERLOOP SUICIDE

This is just ridiculous. When I first saw this move, I simply didn't believe it; it's *so* radically different from anything you've ever seen with two diabolos. The diabolos both come over the stick, whirl round at twice their normal speed in a loop of string, one stick releases, suicides slowly round and is caught, having somehow untangled all the mess! Sounds impossible??? Read on.

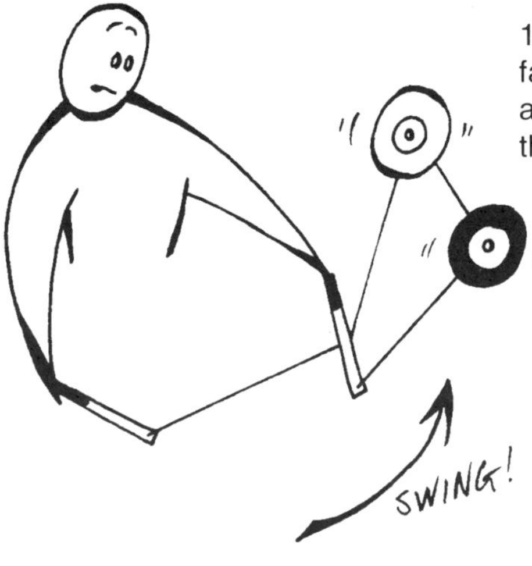

1) Get both diabolos spinning fast, then swing *both* of them into an around the world stopover on the left side.

2) As they come over and land on the string, they will drive themselves 'inside" the loop of string. Quickly!

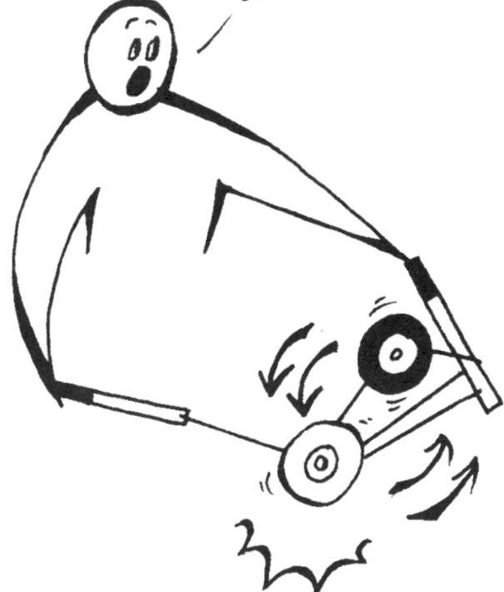

3) Hold this for as long as possible (which is no more than a couple of seconds. Max!)

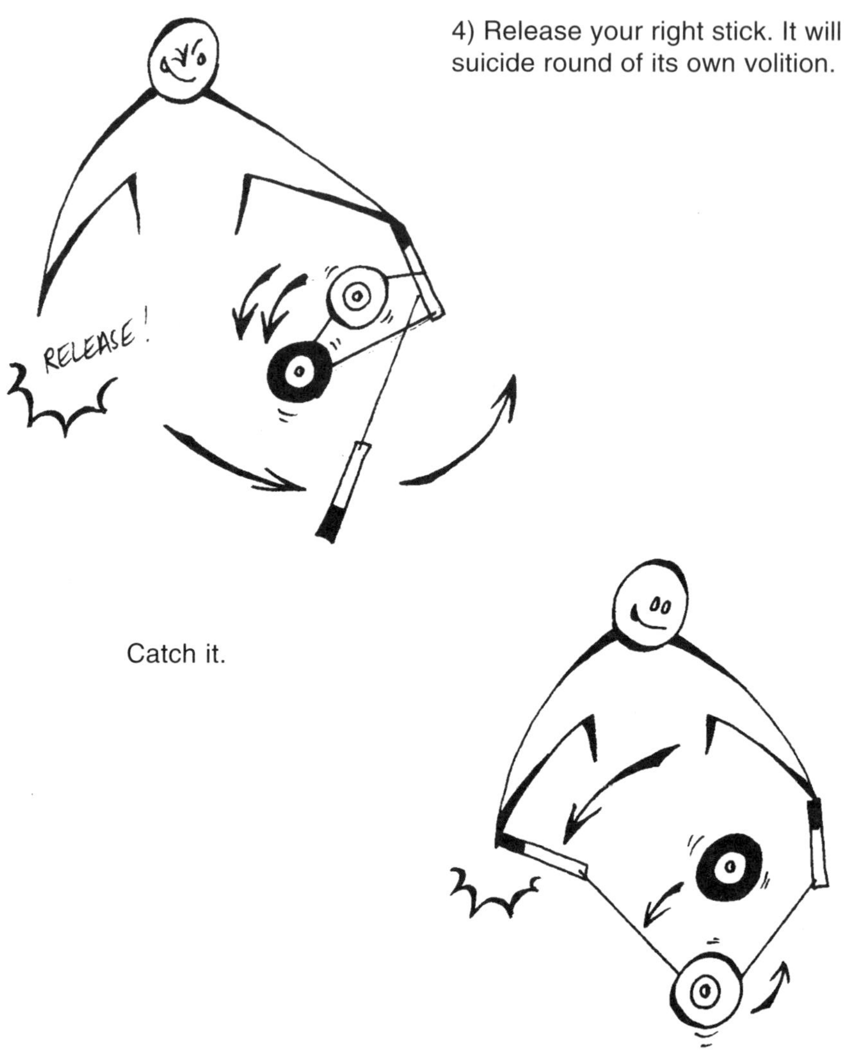

What more can I say? Make sure the diabolos are spinning fast before you start. Make sure you perform the suicide before they have time to collide. Make sure you have plenty of cushions around you whilst learning the trick, just in case you collapse with shock the first time you land it.

MILLS' MESS

One to silence the critics, this ...
How often had I heard the line "bet you can't do Mills' Mess with two diabolos"? More often than you would think, but the most annoying thing was that nobody actually meant it! Well, I decided to put in a bit of work, and here's what I came up with. See what you think.

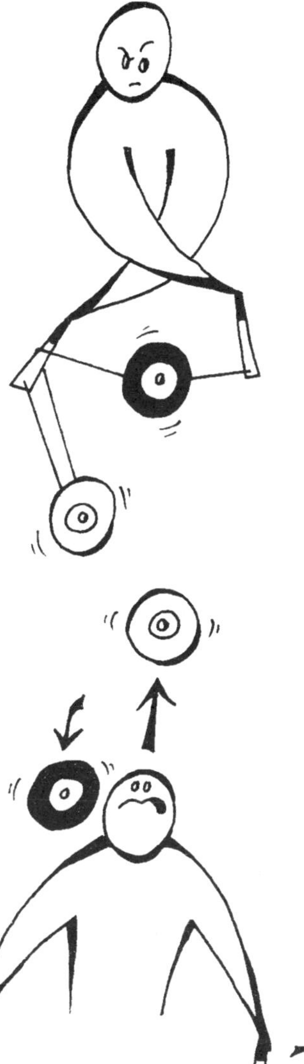

1) From a fast-spinning shuffle, pop one diabolo straight up.

2) Catch it in a 'cross-arm trap" style, arms crossed right over left.

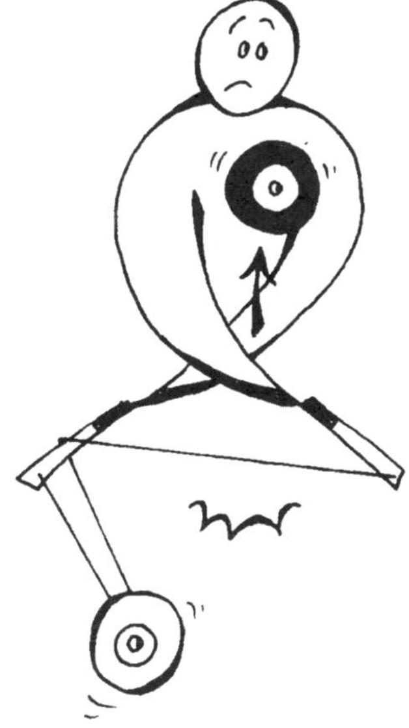

3) Pop this diabolo up.

4) Uncross your arms to throw the second diabolo (not too high.)

5) Catch the first diabolo.

6) Catch the second diabolo in a
cross-arm trap, this time left over
right.

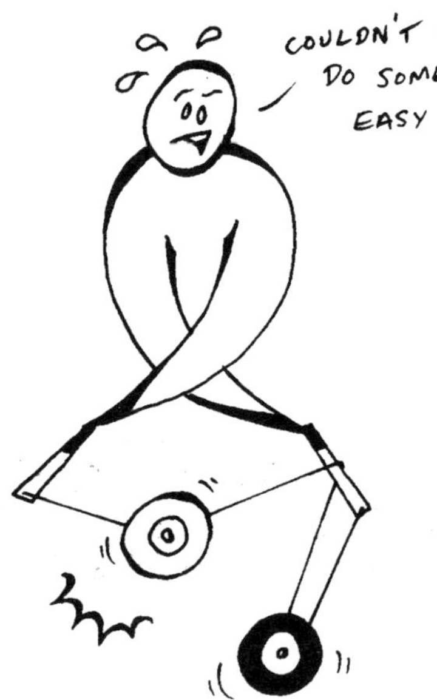

So the sequence goes:
POP-THROW-CATCH-TRAP.
Now repeat in reverse.

Now you have a Mills' Mess
movement with two diabolos
being thrown and caught, prepare
yourself for a torrent of "it can't
be a real Mess without 3
diabolos" comments. Some
people are never satisfied.

PASSING ONE DIABOLO

Passing a diabolo back and forth can not only be relaxing, but also an impressive spectacle for an audience (as it fills the stage so well).
Any old moves can be used during a passing routine, here are just a few of the more unusual ones:

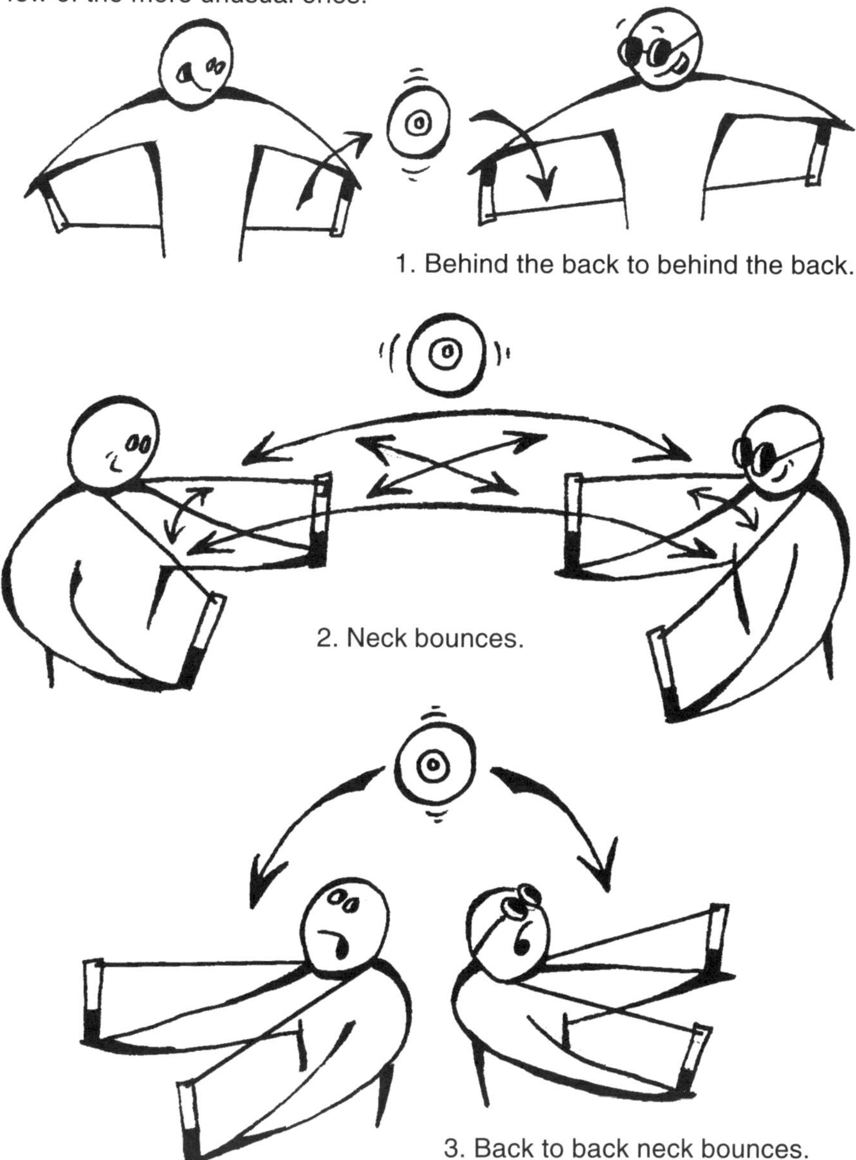

1. Behind the back to behind the back.

2. Neck bounces.

3. Back to back neck bounces.

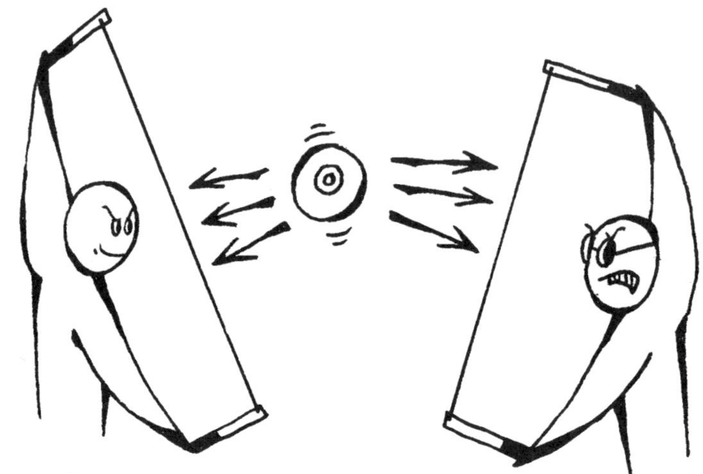

4. Ricochets.

5.Behind the front to behind the (other) front.

6. Hand grind to hand grind!

7. Overhead grind to overhead grind.

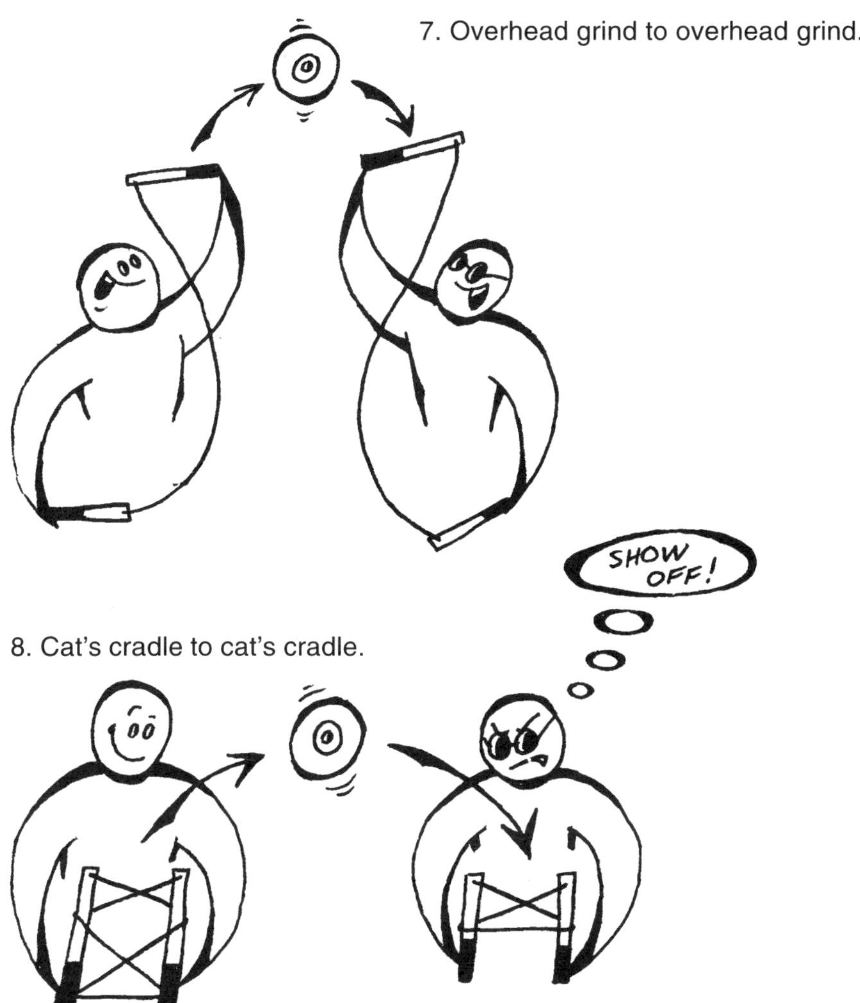

8. Cat's cradle to cat's cradle.

Oh yes, and remember the following pointers too:
1) You and your partner can move/ change places during the routine.
You can even do so acrobatically, should you choose.
2) You can have a lot of fun scaring and psyching each other out with
fake throws.
3) You don't have to pass just the diabolo.
4) For heavens sake, make sure you both spin the diabolo in the same
direction before you start.

PASSING MULTIPLE DIABOLOS

If you enjoy passing one diabolo, why not try passing two? All the "one passing" stuff is now possible with both of you doing it in sync.

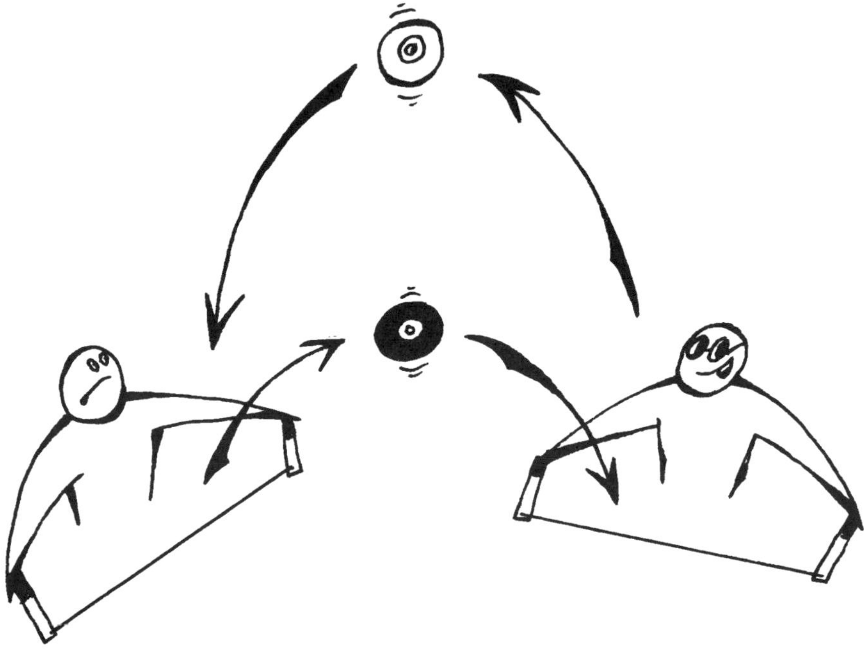

Remember you can pass either "one high one low" (as illustrated) or both at the same height on a slightly different plane to avoid collisions.

You can also try:
Taking turns at doing two diabolo tricks.
Throwing the diabolos vertically and swapping places beneath them.

Three-diabolo passing has obvious similarities to three ball juggling. Here are some of the basic patterns to try first of all:

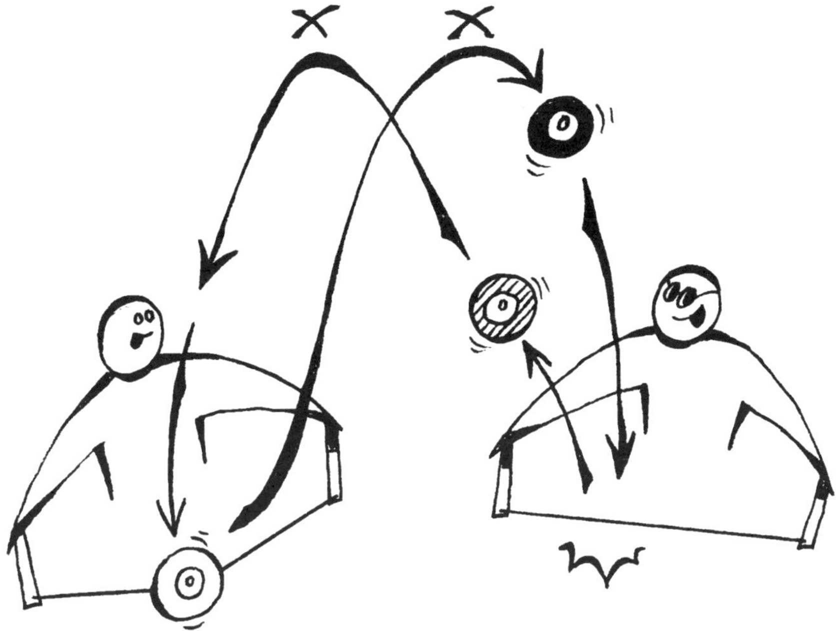

1. Three-diabolo cascade (reverse cascade works too!)

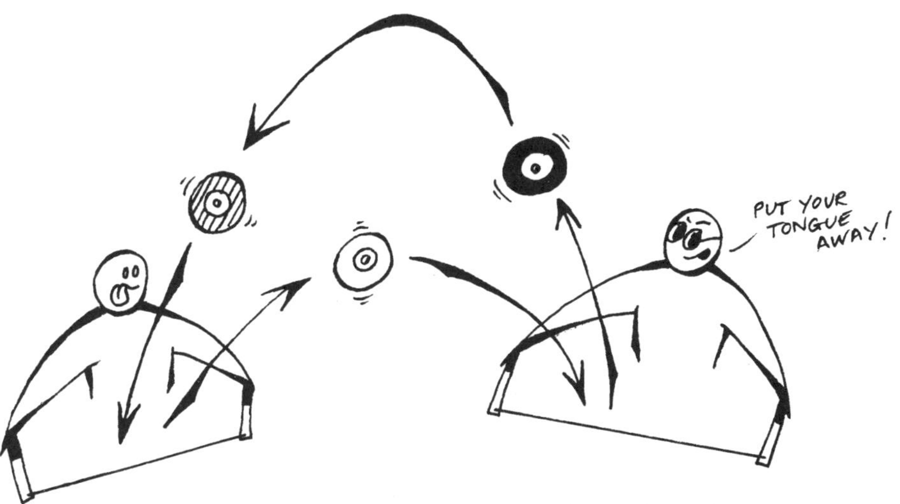

2. Three-diabolo half shower.

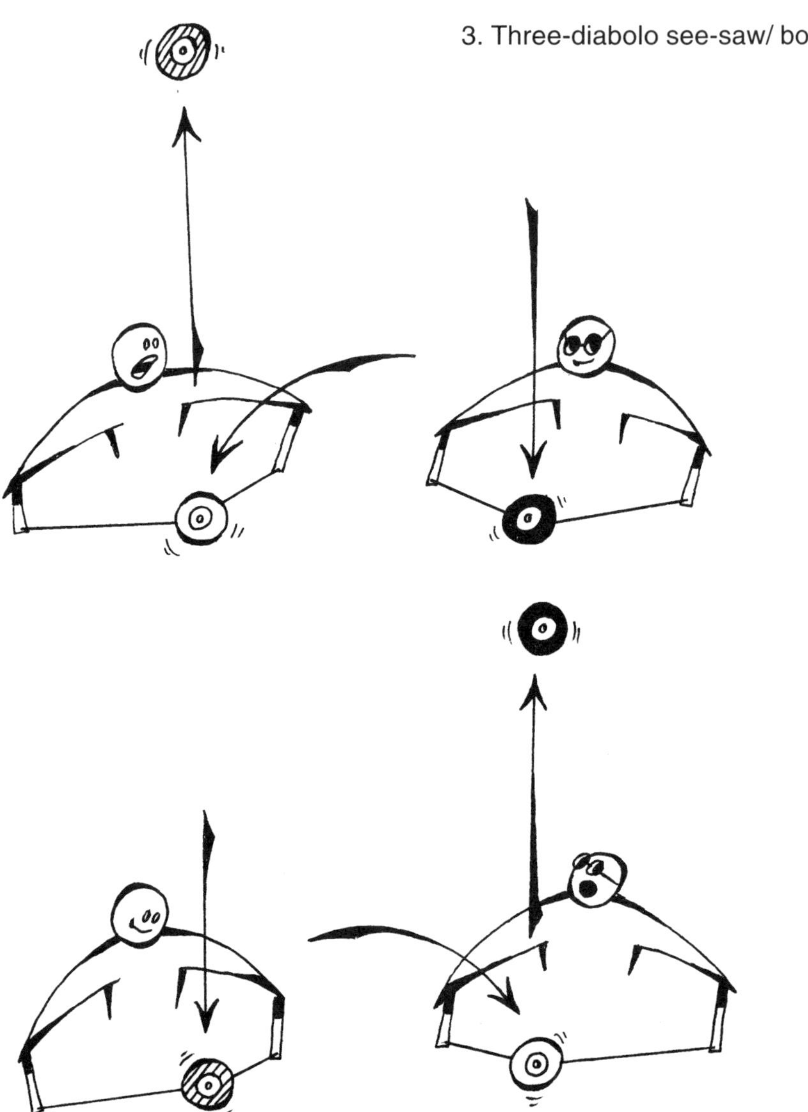

By incorporating two-diabolo shuffles as well, it is possible to get some nice runaround patterns.

Four diabolos? Try two high each with occasional passes. Or even a half shower. And the ultimate? Well, reports have reached my ears of the Chinese performing a FIVE diabolo cascade!

LONG DISTANCE PASSING

This is another silly one which seems to be gaining popularity at juggling conventions these days. The principle is this:
1) One person throws
2) Diabolo travels over distance, the further the better
3) Other person catches
Did I really need to explain that? I don't think so.

As with high throws, be aware of your surroundings. Beaches are generally good, but can be windy (great for throwing one way, not so hot for returning).

Oh, and just in case you want them, here are a few pointers for launch technique. Some folks enjoy the taking-a-run-up-with-a-final-desperate-hurl concept, while others go for a sort of frenzied-whipping-with-sudden-release method. Play around and see what suits you.

And catching? Well, any style which results in the diabolo ending up on the string as opposed to the floor is generally held to be ok. If you get bored, try whip catches.

STRING CLIMB

For some people, the common or garden string climb simply isn't sufficient. So how's about this one:

1) Fix a long string to the ceiling.

2) Get your diabolo spinning as fast as is physically possible.

3) Have someone else ready to loop the bottom of the string round the axle and pull tight.

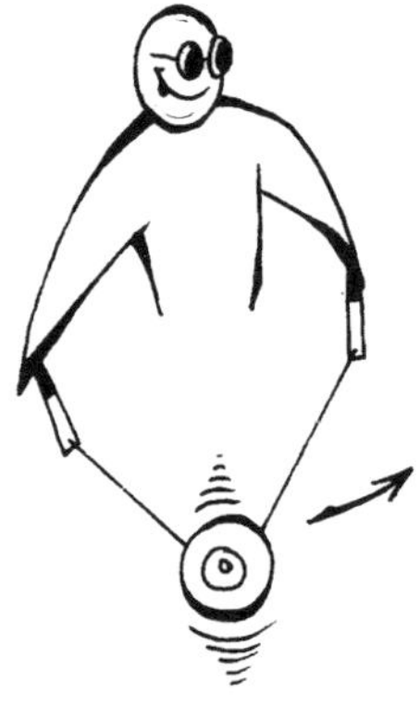

4) Step back and admire, as it rockets skywards.

Just one little problem: how did you manage to fix the string to the ceiling in the first place?

WASHING LINE

Just when you thought the previous trick was inane and pointless ...
String up a length of line between two points (a washing line is ideal for
this, so long as you remove your clothes first. No, no, no - the clothes
on the *line*, you exhibitionist fools!)

1) Put your spinning diabolo on one end.
2) Chase it to the other end.
3) Lift it off again.

Believe it or not, you *will* tire of this eventually. So find yourself a friend
(I know, I know, it isn't easy). Stand at opposite ends of the line, whipping your diabolos into a frenzy. Now set them on each other by send-
ing them along the line. Ta daah! Instant gladiator-type-diabolo-
baiting-warfare-fun-for-all!

Minutes of endless entertainment, guaranteed.

KITE FUN

For this one you will need:
Two people, one diabolo, a single-line kite, preferably of the pocket parafoil variety. Oh, and a windy day, of course.

1) Send the kite up, and have the person with the diabolo stand roughly underneath it.

2) The diabolo is thrown high. The person with the kite tries to catch it on the line.

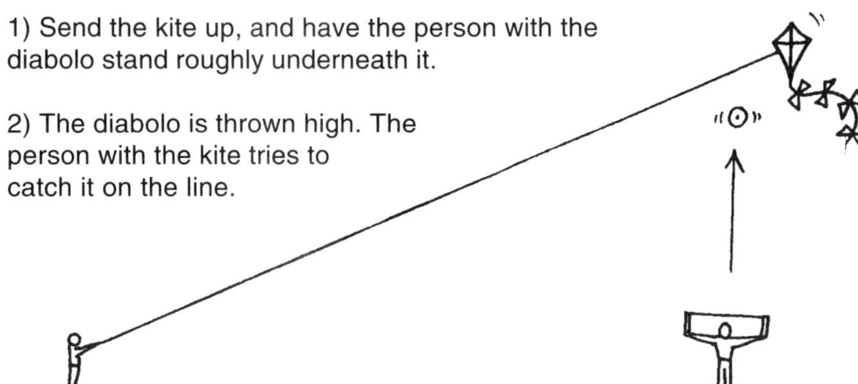

3) Once caught, it will come hurtling down the line. The diabolist must now give chase.

4) Just before it smashes into the knuckles of the person with the kite, they must lift the line sharply to pop the diabolo over their head.

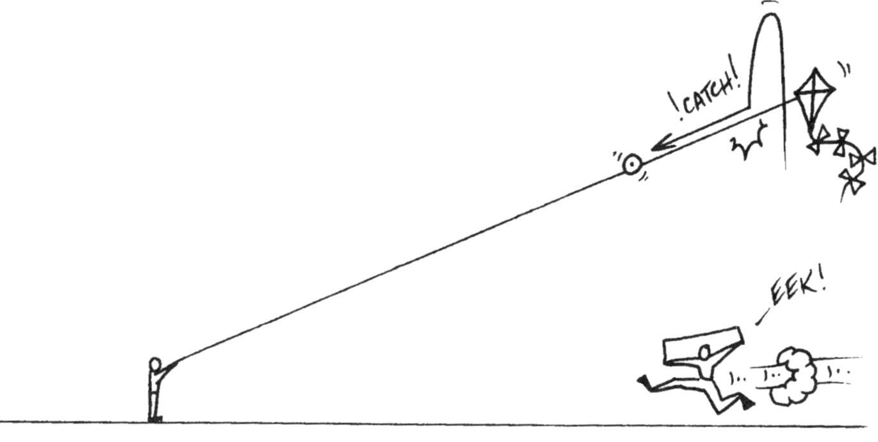

5) The diabolist, who has by now
hopefully arrived, can catch it in
the nick of time.

Now here's a curious little coincidence:
The length of time taken for a diabolo to descend a kite line is roughly
equivalent to the time it takes a diabolist to realise the diabolo has
finally landed on the string, engage their legs and sprint into a head-
long dive just beyond the kite flyer.

If you (somehow) find it all too easy, try it on the beach. Soft sand
makes all the difference, both to sprint times *and* face-first mercy
leaps!

DIABOLOOP

Cast off thy handsticks! Tie your string into a loop. Prepare yourself for something a little different. The diaboloop is a rather unusual concept, which isn't too hard to learn and can offer a pleasant change in both practice and performance.

Firstly, make yourself a loop of string. This can be of any size you want, but a good size to start with seems to be one which reaches from floor to hip and back again.

1) Hold the string, either around your wrists or palms. Put your diabolo on the loop.

2) Swing the diabolo to the left.

3) Now, by moving your hands in a tight circular motion, it's possible to drive the diabolo as it swings around your arms. (This isn't easy to describe: just try it, eh?)

Once you've got used to this, try some of these ideas:

1) All the usual "around both arms" tricks.

2) Around/ over and under legs/ arms/ elbows. (Anything which still keeps two points of the body inside the loop.)

3) Cat's cradles.

4) String climbs.

5) Stopovers (use your thumbs to trap the string.)

If this still doesn't satisfy, why not try it all with an *elastic* loop? Or under UV? Or with *two* diabolos and two loops? Or two diabolos and *one* loop? So many ideas, so little talent ...

HIGH THROW

The high throw is an entire art in itself. A crowd-gathering device to some, a continuing obsession for others.

Don't try it if there is anything overhead, or if there are a combination of high winds and spectators about. Of course, you would think that any rational member of any audience might be able to perceive the threat of any incoming errant throw and avoid it. Not so.

They seem to stand there head thrust back, mouth agape, staring at the rapidly descending diabolo as it plummets towards them. The only thing I can possibly compare it to is the image of a startled rabbit, frozen in the headlights of an oncoming car.

The sound of the impact is uncannily similar too ...

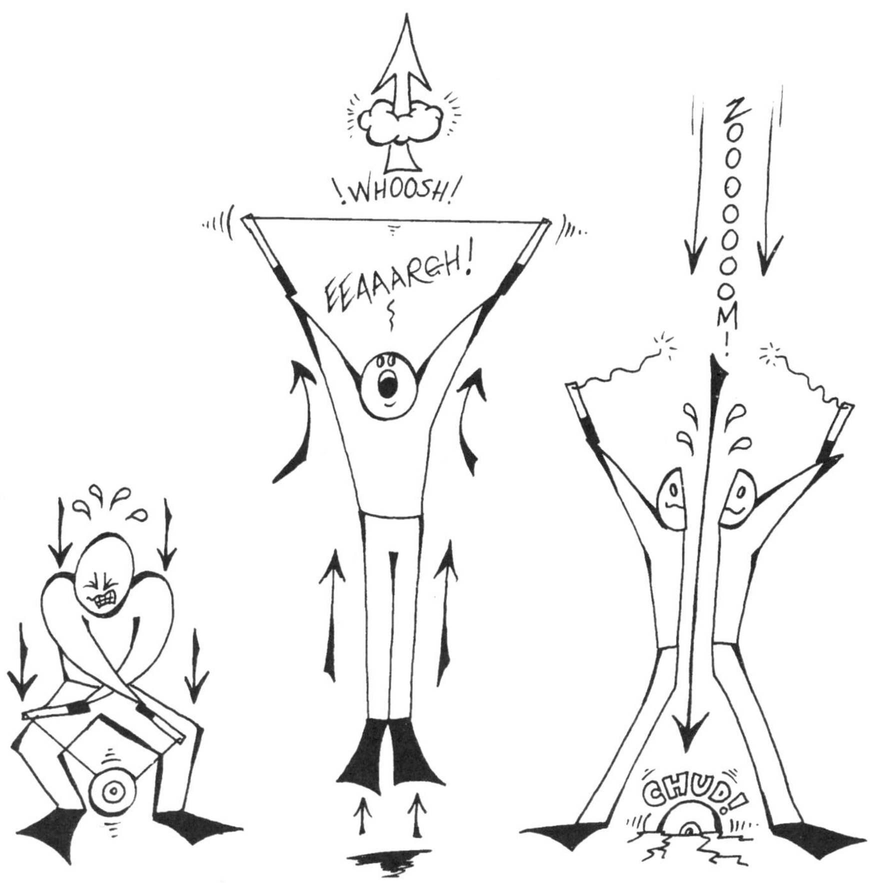

Develop yourself a technique. Everyone has their own personal one, but here's a good one to start you off:
i) Bend your knees. Cross your hands.
ii) Pull the sticks apart fiercely, upwards, and thrust from your legs.
iii) Remember to catch it. It's always more impressive if you catch it.
iv) And finally - watch your head! Seriously, my friend Doug cut his head and was knocked giddy when struck by a high throw during his show. I've laid myself out completely with a high throw of a solid metal fire diabolo. So just be careful, ok?

ULTRA-VIOLET

Under ultra-violet light, much of what is usually "impressive' suddenly isn't. Around the legs and arms, over the face, all lose their visual appeal as the body cannot be seen, and the movements of the prop are all similarly uninspiring. I'm not going to tell you *exactly* what to do trick-wise, that would take all the fun out of it. I would however like to pass on a few helpful hints which should assist you in your quest.

1) Remember that you can have at least four different set-ups:
 i) Only the diabolo visible.
ii) Diabolo and sticks visible (good for suicides).
iii) Diabolo, sticks and string visible (essential for cat's cradles).
iv) All the above, plus gloves so the audience can see your hands.

2) This seems obvious, but remember that you can have other performers on stage invisibly whom you can work with. Remember also that props can easily be made to appear and disappear. The best effects under UV are often those which are unusual or surprising!

3) The moves which tend to look most impressive include:
 i) Wide, fast loops and round the worlds.
ii) Fast suicides.
iii) Nimbly-woven cat's cradles.
iv) Most varieties of whipping.
v) Generally anything with two diabolos.
vi) Ditto three diabolos, of course!

The realms of UV diabolo are still generally unexplored, so get out there and be a pioneer. Oh yes, and if you *really* want to blow the crowd away, I've got one word for you: *Genocide*.

FIRE

The fire diabolo has always had a bit of a bad name, really. People nailing bits of wick to helpless little wooden diabolos, Catherine wheels bolted onto cups, flaming string and heaven knows what other insanity. At last, modern science has caught up with the diabolist's pyrotechnical desires, and there are finally a couple of more user-friendly models on the market. Now I'm sorry if I sound like a bit of a spoilsport, but I'd just like to offer a few guidelines for your own safety:

1) Avoid loose clothing (shell suits are a definite no no!) Tie back any long hair you may happen to have.

2) Find yourself a nice open space, so you're not going to accidentally destroy anything.

3) Get accustomed to the different weight/size/feel of the prop. Practice with it BEFORE YOU LIGHT IT!!!

4) Use paraffin or barbecue lighter fuel, NEVER PETROL.

5) Shake off any excess, don't just try and "spin it off" once lit (yes it DOES look pretty, but isn't exactly safe, is it?)

6) Use kevlar or a similarly fireproof type of string.

7) Make sure any crowd which you have STAND WELL BACK. Unlike other juggling toys, remember that diabolos can be dropped SIDE-WAYS too.

8) After your flame has gone out, cool your diabolo down with a generous bout of whipping.

Ok, ok, I'll get down from my pulpit. Now that you're more than aware that fire deserves respect, here are a few pointers as to which tricks look the best:

1) High throws (crash helmets advised!)

2) Large loops and round the worlds.

3) Body moves close to the body.

Oh, and finally, remember that it always looks better in the dark. As many of us do.

ALTERNATIVE WHIPPING

It's very easy to get bored with normal side-side whipping. It can often become a bit of a chore if you're learning a new trick which requires large amounts of spin. So here are three alternatives to keep you amused as you strive for those high RPMs.

VERTICAL WHIPPING

This one is quite easy. It's exactly the same as normal whipping, but flipped on its side. Practice whipping as usual, and every now and again try lifting *up* (rather than pulling to the side) with your right hand, and pulling down. Eventually you should be able to whip with the diabolo moving at a 45 degree angle. With time and effort this can be near vertical. (NB Use only *inside* strokes).

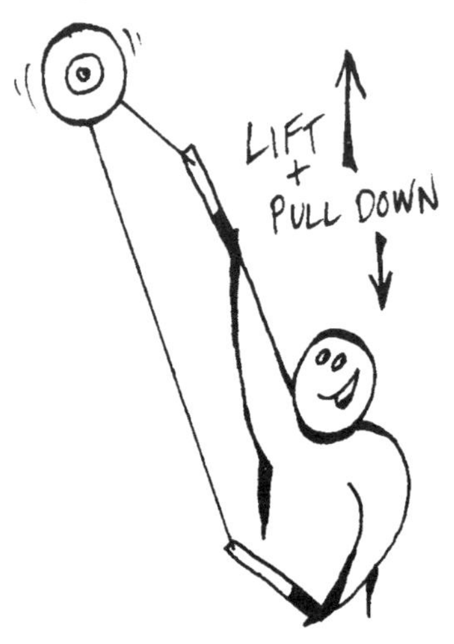

CHINESE WHIPPING

A classic one this, as used for centuries by (you've guessed it) the Chinese. You must have a *clean, unfrayed string* for this to work, otherwise it will tangle up. So get rid of that bit of raggedy old wax-encrusted hemp you've been using, right?
1) Loop the string around the axle, as for a string climb.
2) Flick firmly up and down with the right hand to accelerate.

UMBRELLA WHIPPING

As popularised by Jochen Schell. A fast, crazy whipping which travels laterally to and fro above the head. It takes some time to perfect, but here's the easiest way I've found to learn it.

1) Practice the beginners round the world; where the diabolo is swung in a circle in front of you, twisting the string. Then swing it back the other way to untwist it.

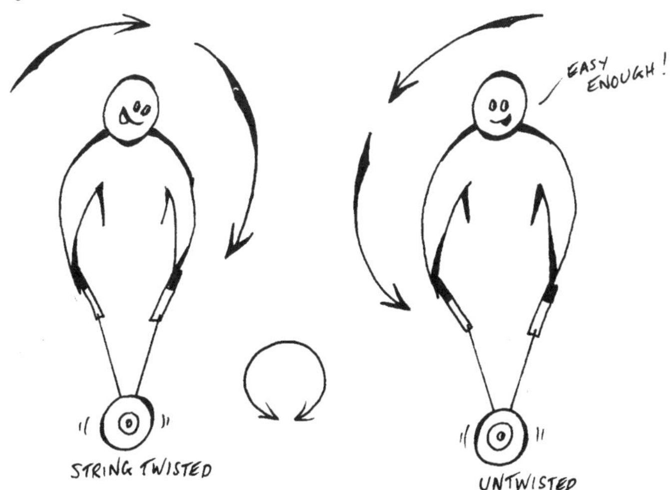

2) Now do the same, but a little faster. As you swing to the left, step slightly to the left; as you swing right, step right. The diabolo should now be following an arc pattern, as opposed to the previous circular one.

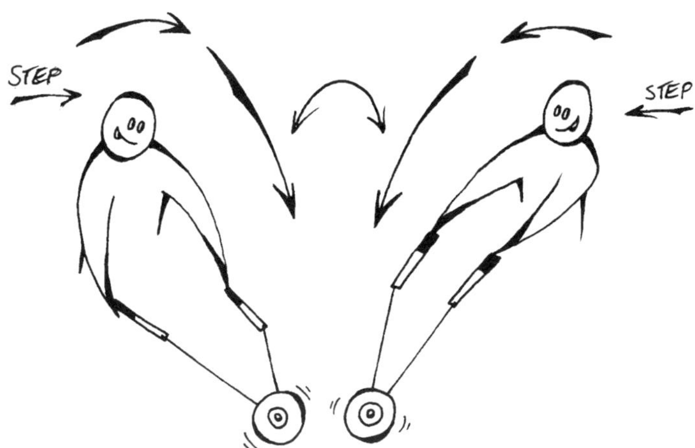

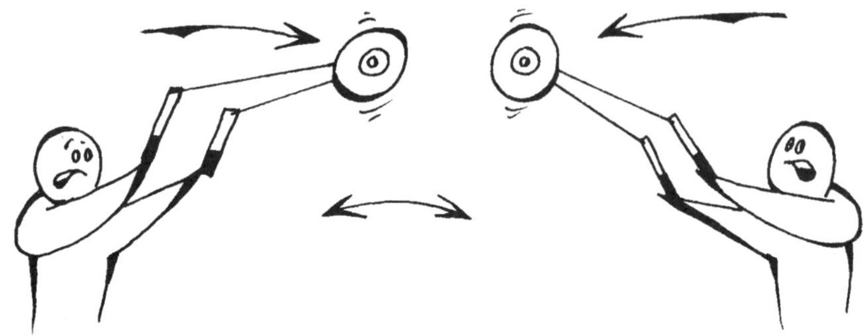

3) Do it faster still. Hold your handsticks up at face level. You should now, with practice, be pulling the diabolo back and forth rapidly in a near-horizontal overhead trajectory.

And if *none of* the above alternative whips seem good enough for you, either:

i) Make up your own, or
ii) Fit your diabolo with a motor.

DRIVING

Driving is a method by which you keep the diabolo spinning through endless combinations without ever having to stop and whip. Sounds too good to be true? Well ...

Almost any trick which is circular in motion can be driven. Some, you may have noticed yourself, seem to drive themselves anyway (such as around the leg).

Around the leg is a good example to start off with. As the diabolo goes around the leg try pushing *down* with the right hand every time you catch the diabolo. With practice you should be able to actually accelerate the diabolo as the trick progresses.

Now try and learn it with around the worlds. Each time the diabolo passes between your arms push *down* with your right hand. At first you will probably have little success as it is purely a feel thing, but you will get it in time. Every move has a different driving point, so experiment to find out what they are.

Anyway, as most sequences contain circular moves, eventually you should be able to drive any combination without having to bother about whipping.

COMBINATIONS

Once you start combining moves into sequences, you open up a whole new realm. You suddenly realise that three or four relatively easy moves seamlessly strung together can look just as impressive (if not more so) than one extra-hard move.

The variety of different combinations are, of course, infinite. And as most of the fun comes from making them up for yourself, I'm not going to give you any specific ones to learn. Here to help you on your way, however, are a few tips.

1) Round the worlds are the best sorts of moves to start learning combinations with as they flow easily and smoothly into one another.

2) If you wish to change the direction of swing in a sequence, a round the world stopover or a gentle low throw are smoothest.

3) The easiest bodymove combinations are generally around the leg (around leg, figure 8, one-handed, grind carry, suicide, etc).

4) Try to end any combinations with a finishing touch, such as a nice cat's cradle or some sort of suicide.

5) Make sure you don't run out of spin half way through.

ROUTINES

The *last* thing I want to do is tell you how to perform. A routine is a personal thing and everyone has different opinions as to what they want to do. Here, however, are ten pointers which should be helpful if you are thinking of putting together a piece.

1) If you're going to use music, *don't* just choose something because it's your favourite song. A good tip is to practice with lots of different pieces of music and eventually you will get a feel for which rhythms and tempos suit your particular style.

2) Don't neglect other considerations such as costume and lighting. You may think this is a little over-the-top for your first routine, but even the tiniest of touches can make all the difference.

3) Remember that the hardest tricks aren't always the most impressive to the layman. (High throws and string climbs are proof of that!)

4) Keep spare handsticks and a diabolo in the wings. Accidents and non-magic knots *do* happen.

5) Don't just stand there like a scarecrow! I know that the diabolo is a small prop but a good performer can fill any stage easily. Move!!!

6) Have a good mixture of skills. Changing between wide moves (round the worlds and suicides), tight moves (around the body) and static moves (grinds and cradles) provides contrast and variety.

7) With moves like cat's cradles and magic knots, *show* them to the audience. Let your crowd have the time to appreciate them before you move on.

8) Constant whipping can look very dull and break down a flow of a routine. Use the alternative whipping and driving from the previous sections to keep things going. (Remember that even the different types of whipping can be performed with style and movement).

9) Symmetry is important. If you only perform each trick on your favourite side, the whole thing will look lop-sided.

10) Make your final trick big on impact and 100% on success rate. Hitting or missing your last move can make all the difference between an adulatory and a sympathetic reception! Popular finishes include grind to a halt, chinese knot, duicide or (if you're brave) one of the whip catch family ...

2) Use the smallest diabolo you can find. It will be harder to catch, but the height you gain can be truly breathtaking. It's also a bit safer should it clobber you one.

FURTHER AND BEYOND

What? You've finished already? You can't have learned all those tricks so quickly? Look, this book took me over a year to compile so don't you *dare* come complaining to me that it isn't sufficient!

Seriously though, if you have managed to learn everything in this book, then there is little else that I can offer. At the time that I'm writing this, there really isn't much more which is considered *possible*!

But ...

The soundest advice which I can offer you is to think of the diabolo in terms of five different props: sticks, string, diabolo, body and most importantly mind.

Each can be manipulated or utilised in a myriad of different ways, but as long as you don't concentrate on the first four to the exclusion of the last one, you may be surprised what you come up with. Using your brain can often be infinitely more productive than endless practice sessions. Or endlessly ploughing through books of tricks for that matter.

PS Oh yes, and for goodness sake remember to have fun. It's only a toy, y'know!

THANKS AND ACKNOWLEDGEMENTS

These books don't just slide out of my brain and onto your bookshelves on their own, y'know. All of the following people have somehow been involved along the way. This is my chance to thank them for all their support.

Stewart Hutton, my glutton-for-punishment publisher (it's ok, I PROMISE there'll be no more after this!)

Samantha, purely and simply for putting up with me.

Stuart Fell for the Star.

Guy Heathcote for the Chinese Knot.

Bruce Wilson for Stick Switch Grind Behind.

Robert Biegler for the Overcide, the Flipcide and (gulp!) the Genocide. Truly he is a diabolunatic of the highest order.

Neil Ramsey for Cross Arm Traps.

Brendan Brolly for Behind the Back Scoop and Around Both Arms Fig.8 Reverse.

Fritz Grobe for Around Crossed Arms.

R. Allen for the Alternative Floor Start.

Dave From Sheffield for the Hyperloop Suicide.

Miles Ford and Ewan Buchanan (who else!) for, you've guessed it, that *?!&#* kite trick.

And finally Caroline for the Hair Grind.

Anyone else whom I've forgotten, then thank you too. From the heart of my bottom. You're all mad.

Further diabolical reading matter from Donald Grant ...

ISBN 0 9520300 5 5

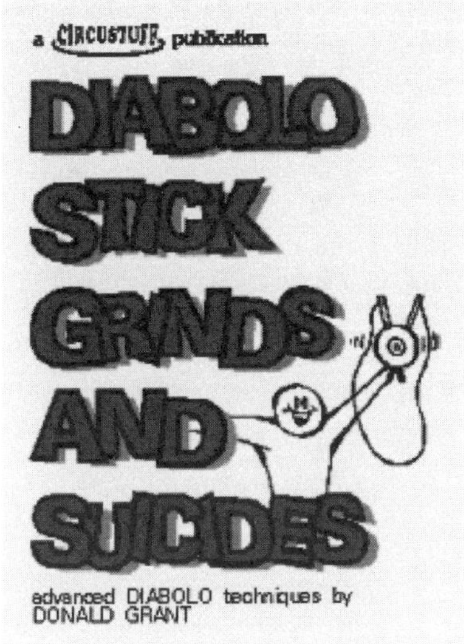

ISBN 0 9520300 0 4

ISBN 0 9520300 1 2

ISBN 0 9520300 2 0

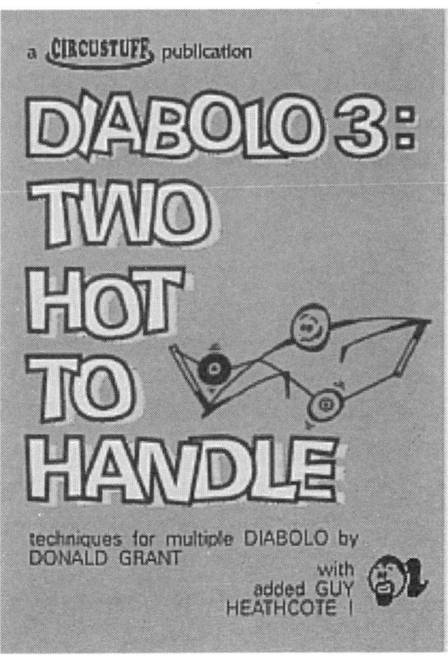